TO

FROM

DATE

God's Priorities
FOR YOUR LIFE

FOR MEN

HENDRICKSON PUBLISHERS

God's Priorities for Your Life for Men

©2006 Hendrickson Publishers, Inc.
P. O. Box 3473
Peabody, MA 01961

ISBN-13: 978-1-59856-133-3
ISBN-10: 1-59856-133-2

Printed in the United States of America

First printing—August 2006

Except for quotations from Scripture, the quoted ideas expressed in this book are not, in all cases, exact quotations, as some have been edited for clarity and brevity. In all cases, the author has attempted to maintain the speaker's original intent. In some cases, quoted material for this book was obtained from secondary sources, primarily print media. While every effort was made to ensure the accuracy of these sources, the accuracy cannot be guaranteed. For additions, deletions, corrections, or clarifications in future editions of this text, please write Hendrickson Publishers, Inc.

Scriptures marked NIV® are from the Holy Bible, New International Version®. Copyright © 1973, 1978, 1984 by International Bible Society. Used by permission of Zondervan Publishing House. All rights reserved.

Scriptures marked NASB are taken from the New American Standard Bible®. © Copyright The Lockman Foundation 1960, 1962, 1963, 1968, 1971, 1972, 1973, 1975, 1977, 1995. Used by permission. (www.Lockman.org).

Scriptures marked NKJV are taken from the New King James Version®. Copyright © 1982 by Thomas Nelson, Inc. Used by permission. All rights reserved.

Scriptures marked NLT are taken from the Holy Bible, New Living Translation, copyright © 1996. Used by permission of Tyndale House Publishers, Inc., Wheaton, Illinois 60189. All rights reserved.

Scriptures marked NCV are quoted from The Holy Bible, New Century Version, copyright © 1987, 1988, 1991 by Word Publishing, Nashville, Tennessee 37214. Used by permission.

Scriptures marked KJV are taken from the King James Version.

Scripture quotations marked MSG are taken from The Message. Copyright © by Eugene H. Peterson 1993, 1994, 1995. Used by permission of NavPress Publishing Group.

Scripture quotations marked ICB are taken from the International Children's Bible, New Century Version © 1986, 1988 by Word Publishing, Nashville, Tennessee 37214. Used by permission.

Scripture quotations marked TLB are taken from The Living Bible copyright © 1971. Used by permission of Tyndale House Publishers, Inc., Wheaton, Illinois 60189. All rights reserved.

Scripture quotations marked Holman CSB are taken from the Holman Christian Standard Bible®, Copyright © 1999, 2000, 2002, 2003 by Holman Bible Publishers. Used by permission. Holman Christian Standard Bible®, Holman CSB®, and HCSB® are federally registered trademarks of Holman Bible Publishers.

Cover Design by Kim Russell / Wahoo Designs
Page Layout by Bart Dawson

God's Priorities

FOR YOUR LIFE

FOR MEN

TABLE OF CONTENTS

INTRODUCTION

How many decisions do you make in a typical day? When you stop to think about it, you make thousands of choices, usually without too much forethought. Of course, most of these choices are relatively small ones, like what to do at a given moment, or what to say, or how to direct your thoughts. Occasionally, you will face major decisions, like choosing to be a Christian, or choosing a profession, or choosing a spouse. But whatever choices you face, whether they're big, little, or somewhere in between, you can be sure of this: the quality of your choices will make an enormous difference in the quality of your life.

Your choices are shaped by your priorities. Simply put, your priorities determine, to a surprising extent, the quality of the decisions you make and the direction that your life will take. And that's why the ideas in this book are so important.

This book addresses Christian values that can—and should—shape your life. You may find it helpful to read the book from cover to cover, or you may decide to scan the Table of Contents and then turn to chapters that seem particularly important to you. Either way, the ideas on these pages will serve to remind you of God's commandments, God's promises, God's love, and God's Son—all things that are crucially important as you establish priorities for the next stage of your life's journey.

Whose values do you hold most dear: society's values or God's values? When you decide to make God's priorities your priorities, you will receive His abundance and His peace. When you make God a full partner in every aspect of your life, He will lead you along the proper path: His path. When you allow God to direct your steps, He will honor you with spiritual blessings that are simply too numerous to count. So, as you make your next important decision, pause to consider the values that serve as the starting point for that decision. When you do, your decision-making will be vastly improved . . . and so will your life.

Jesus Christ is the first and last, author and finisher,
beginning and end, alpha and omega,
and by Him all other things hold together.
He must be first or nothing. God never comes next!

Vance Havner

Let us fix our eyes on Jesus, the author
and perfecter of our faith, who for the joy
set before him endured the cross,
scorning its shame, and sat down
at the right hand of the throne of God.

Hebrews 12:2 NIV

God's Priorities for Your Life

First pay attention to me, and then relax.
Now you can take it easy—you're in good hands.

Proverbs 1:33 MSG

On your daily to-do list, all items are not created equal: Certain tasks are extremely important while others are not. Therefore, it's imperative that you prioritize your daily activities and complete each task in the approximate order of its importance.

The principle of doing first things first is simple in theory but more complicated in practice. Well-meaning family, friends, and coworkers have a way of making unexpected demands upon your time. Furthermore, each day has it own share of minor emergencies; these urgent matters tend to draw your attention away from more important ones. On paper, prioritizing is simple, but to act upon those priorities in the real world requires maturity, patience, determination, and balance.

If you fail to prioritize your day, life will automatically do the job for you. So your choice is simple: prioritize or be prioritized. It's a choice that will help determine the quality of your life.

If you're having trouble balancing the many demands of everyday living, perhaps you've been trying to organize your life according to your own priorities, not God's. A better strategy, of course, is to take your daily obligations and place them in the hands of the One who created you. To do so, you must prioritize your day according to God's commandments, and you must seek His will and His wisdom in all matters. Then, you can face the coming day with the assurance that the same God who created our universe out of nothingness will help you place first things first in your own life.

Are you living a balanced life that allows time for worship, for family, for work, for exercise, and a little time left over for you? Or do you feel overworked, under-appreciated, overwhelmed, and underpaid? If your to-do list is "maxed out" and your energy is on the wane, it's time to restore a sense of balance to your life. You can do so by turning the concerns and the priorities of this day over to God—prayerfully, earnestly, and often. Then, you must listen for His answer . . . and trust the answer He gives.

PRIORITIES FOR MY LIFE

Making Time for God: Our days are filled to the brim with obligations and priorities, but no priority is greater than our obligation to our Creator. Let's make sure that we give Him the time He deserves, not only on Sundays, but also on every other day of the week.

TIMELESS WISDOM FOR GODLY LIVING

Often our lives are strangled by things that don't ultimately matter.

Grady Nutt

How important it is for us—young and old—to live as if Jesus would return any day—to set our goals, make our choices, raise our children, and conduct business with the perspective of the imminent return of our Lord.

Gloria Gaither

No horse gets anywhere until he is harnessed. No life ever grows great until it is focused, dedicated, disciplined.

Harry Emerson Fosdick

And I pray this: that your love will keep on growing in knowledge and every kind of discernment, so that you can determine what really matters and can be pure and blameless in the day of Christ.
Philippians 1:9 Holman CSB

The most important business I'm engaged in ought to be the Lord's business. If it ain't, I need to get off and classify myself and see whose side I'm on.

Jerry Clower

MORE WORDS FROM GOD'S WORD

The thing you should want most is God's kingdom and doing what God wants. Then all these other things you need will be given to you.

Matthew 6:33 NCV

He said to them all, "If anyone desires to come after Me, let him deny himself, and take up his cross daily, and follow Me. For whoever desires to save his life will lose it, but whoever loses his life for My sake will save it."

Luke 9:23-24 NKJV

In a race, everyone runs but only one person gets first prize . . . to win the contest you must deny yourselves many things that would keep you from doing your best.

1 Corinthians 9:24-25 TLB

MY PRIORITIES FOR LIFE

| | Check Your Priority | |
High	Med.	Low

I understand the importance of reviewing my priorities frequently.

— — —

On my priority list, I put God first and my family second.

— — —

I place a high value on doing important tasks first and easy tasks later.

— — —

Discovering God's Purpose . . . And Doing It

In Him we were also made His inheritance,
predestined according to the purpose of the One who works out
everything in agreement with the decision of His will.

Ephesians 1:11 Holman CSB

Life is best lived on purpose. And purpose, like everything else in the universe, begins in the heart of God. Whether you realize it or not, God has a direction for your life, a divine calling, a path along which He intends to lead you. When you welcome God into your heart and establish a genuine relationship with Him, He will begin—and He will continue—to make His purposes known.

Each morning, as the sun rises in the East, you welcome a new day, one that is filled to the brim with opportunities, with possibilities, and with God. As you contemplate God's blessings in your own life, you should prayerfully seek His guidance for the day ahead.

Discovering God's unfolding purpose for your life is a daily journey, a journey guided by the teachings of God's Holy Word. As you reflect upon God's promises and upon the meaning that those promises hold for you, ask God to lead you throughout the coming day. Let your Heavenly Father direct your steps; concentrate on what God wants you to do now, and leave the distant future in hands that are far more capable than your own: His hands.

Sometimes, God's intentions will be clear to you; other times, God's plan will seem uncertain at best. But even on those difficult days when you are unsure which way to turn, you must never lose sight of these overriding facts: God created you for a reason; He has important work for you to do; and He's waiting patiently for you to do it. So why not begin today?

We must always invite Jesus to be the navigator of our plans,
desires, wills, and emotions, for He is the way,
the truth, and the life.

Bill Bright

PRIORITIES FOR MY LIFE

God still has a wonderful plan for your life. And the time to start looking for that plan—and living it—is now. (Psalm 16:11)

TIMELESS WISDOM FOR GODLY LIVING

Let your fellowship with the Father and with the Lord Jesus Christ have as its one aim and object a life of quiet, determined, unquestioning obedience.

Andrew Murray

The place where God calls you is the place where your deep gladness and the world's deep hunger meet.

Frederick Buechner

Nothing in this world is without meaning.

A. W. Tozer

> *To everything there is a season,*
> *a time for every purpose under heaven.*
> Ecclesiastes 3:1 NKJV

The born-again Christian sees life not as a blurred, confused, meaningless mass, but as something planned and purposeful.

Billy Graham

MORE WORDS FROM GOD'S WORD

I urge you to live a life worthy of the calling you have received.

Ephesians 4:1 NIV

Whatever you do, do everything for God's glory.

1 Corinthians 10:31 Holman CSB

The lines of purpose in your lives never grow slack, tightly tied as they are to your future in heaven, kept taut by hope.

Colossians 1:5 MSG

There is one thing I always do. Forgetting the past and straining toward what is ahead, I keep trying to reach the goal and get the prize for which God called me . . .

Philippians 3:13–14 NCV

MY PRIORITIES FOR LIFE

	Check Your Priority		
	High	Med.	Low
I understand the importance of discovering God's unfolding purpose for my life.	—	—	—
I consult God on matters great and small.	—	—	—
I pray about my plans for the future.	—	—	—
I remain open to the opportunities and challenges that God places before me.	—	—	—

Success
According to God

Success, success to you, and success to those who help you,
for your God will help you . . . .

1 Chronicles 12:18 NIV

Wouldn't it be nice if we could uncover a few "secrets" to success? But we can't. Why? Because the keys to a successful life aren't really secrets at all—the keys to success are simply those good, old-fashioned, common-sense principles that we've heard since we were children. And the good news is this: those principles really do work.

Do you want to be successful? Then here are a few things you should do:

1. Put God First . . . in every aspect of your life, including your career.
2. Wherever You Happen To Be, Be the Best You Can Be: Giving your best is habit-forming, so give your best every time you go to work.
3. Keep Learning: The future belongs to those who are willing to do the work that's required to prepare for it.
4. Have Patience and Perseverance . . . Rome wasn't built in a day, and the same goes for your life.

5. When You Make a Wrong Turn and Find Yourself at the End of a Dead-end Street . . . turn around sooner rather than later.

And above all, remember this: genuine success has little to do with fame or fortune; it has everything to do with God's gift of love and His promise of salvation.

If you have accepted Christ as your personal Savior, you are already a towering success in the eyes of God, but there is still more that you can do. Your task—as a believer who has been touched by the Creator's grace—is to accept the spiritual abundance and peace that He offers through the person of His Son. Then, you can share the healing message of God's love and His abundance with a world that desperately needs both. When you do, you will have reached the pinnacle of success.

Success in any field is costly, but the man who will
pay the price can have it. The laws of success operate also
in the higher field of the soul—spiritual greatness has its price.

A. W. Tozer

PRIORITIES FOR MY LIFE

Have Faith and Get Busy: Here's a time-tested formula for success: have faith in God and do the work.

TIMELESS WISDOM FOR GODLY LIVING

There is nothing more important in any life than the constantly enjoyed presence of the Lord. There is nothing more vital, for without it we shall make mistakes, and without it we shall be defeated.

Alan Redpath

Every achievement worth remembering is stained with the blood of diligence and scarred by the wounds of disappointment.

Charles Swindoll

True success is promised to those who meditate on God's Word, who think deeply on Scripture, not just at one time each day, but at moments throughout the day and night. They meditate so much that Scripture saturates their conversation.

Donald S. Whitney

But as for you, be strong and do not give up, for your work will be rewarded.
2 Chronicles 15:7 NIV

The higher the ideal, the more work is required to accomplish it. Do not expect to become a great success in life if you are not willing to work for it.

Father Flanagan

MORE WORDS FROM GOD'S WORD

Let us not become weary in doing good, for at the proper time we will reap a harvest if we do not give up.

Galatians 6:9 NIV

You need to persevere so that when you have done the will of God, you will receive what he has promised.

Hebrews 10:36 NIV

The one who understands a matter finds success, and the one who trusts in the Lord will be happy.

Proverbs 16:20 Holman CSB

The one who acquires good sense loves himself; one who safeguards understanding finds success.

Proverbs 19:8 Holman CSB

MY PRIORITIES FOR LIFE

I believe God did not create me for a life of mediocrity; He has bigger things in mind.

I believe success requires that I know God's plan for my life.

I believe success comes when I work hard to accomplish my goals.

Check Your Priority		
High	Med.	Low
—	—	—
—	—	—
—	—	—

Using Your Gifts to Serve

Think of yourselves the way Christ Jesus thought of himself.
He had equal status with God but didn't think so much of himself
that he had to cling to the advantages of that status no matter what.
Not at all. When the time came, he set aside the privileges of deity and
took on the status of a slave, became human! Having become human,
he stayed human. It was an incredibly humbling process.
He didn't claim special privileges. Instead he lived a selfless,
obedient life and then died a selfless, obedient death,
and the worst kind of death at that: a crucifixion.

Philippians 2:5-8 MSG

We live in a world that glorifies power, prestige, fame, and money. But the words of Jesus teach us that the most esteemed men and women are not the widely acclaimed leaders of society; the most esteemed among us are the humble servants of society.

When we experience success, it's easy to puff out our chests and proclaim, "I did that!" But it's wrong. Whatever "it" is, God did it, and He deserves the credit. As Christians, we have been refashioned and saved by Jesus Christ, and that salvation came not because of our own good works but because of God's grace.

Dietrich Bonhoeffer was correct when he observed, "It is very easy to overestimate the importance of our own achievements in comparison with what we owe others." In other words, reality breeds humility.

Are you willing to become a humble servant for Christ? Are you willing to pitch in and make the world a better place, or are you determined to keep all your blessings to yourself. The answers to these questions will determine the quantity and the quality of the service your render to God—and to His children.

Today, you may feel the temptation to take more than you give. You may be tempted to withhold your generosity. Or you may be tempted to build yourself up in the eyes of your friends. Resist these temptations. Instead, serve your friends quietly and without fanfare. Find a need and fill it . . . humbly. Lend a helping hand . . . anonymously. Share a word of kindness . . . with quiet sincerity. As you go about your daily activities, remember that the Savior of all humanity made Himself a servant, and you, as His follower, must do no less.

Carve your name on hearts, not on marble.

C. H. Spurgeon

PRIORITIES FOR MY LIFE

Jesus modeled servanthood. Follow His example, even when service to others requires sacrifice on your part.

TIMELESS WISDOM FOR GODLY LIVING

Do things for others and you'll find your self-consciousness evaporating like morning dew on a Missouri cornfield in July.

Dale Carnegie

Christians are like the flowers in a garden: they have upon them the dew of heaven, which, being shaken by the wind, they let fall at each other's roots, whereby they are jointly nourished.

John Bunyan

We are only fully alive when we're helping others.

Rick Warren

> *But a Samaritan, as he traveled, came where the man was;*
> *and when he saw him, he took pity on him. He went*
> *to him and bandaged his wounds, pouring on oil and wine.*
> *Then he put the man on his own donkey,*
> *took him to an inn and took care of him.*
> *Luke 10:33-34 NIV*

I can usually sense that a leading is from the Holy Spirit when it calls me to humble myself, serve somebody, encourage somebody or give something away. Very rarely will the evil one lead us to do those kind of things.

Bill Hybels

MORE WORDS FROM GOD'S WORD

Suppose a brother or a sister is without clothes and daily food. If one of you says to him, "Go, I wish you well; keep warm and well fed," but does nothing about his physical needs, what good is it?

James 2:15-16 NIV

The greatest among you will be your servant. For whoever exalts himself will be humbled, and whoever humbles himself will be exalted.

Matthew 23:11-12 NIV

Those of us who are strong and able in the faith need to step in and lend a hand to those who falter, and not just do what is most convenient for us. Strength is for service, not status. Each one of us needs to look after the good of the people around us, asking ourselves, "How can I help?"

Romans 15:1-2 MSG

MY PRIORITIES FOR LIFE

Christ was a humble servant, and I value the importance of following His example.

I believe that greatness in God's kingdom relates to service, not status.

I am proactive in my search to find ways to help others.

Check Your Priority		
High	Med.	Low
—	—	—
—	—	—
—	—	—

Pleasing God First

Do you think I am trying to make people accept me?
No, God is the One I am trying to please. Am I trying to please people?
If I still wanted to please people, I would not be a servant of Christ.

Galatians 1:10 NCV

When God made you, He equipped you with an array of talents and abilities that are uniquely yours. It's up to you to discover those talents and to use them, but sometimes the world will encourage you to do otherwise. At times, society will attempt to cubbyhole you, to standardize you, and to make you fit into a particular, preformed mold. Perhaps God has other plans.

Sometimes, because you're not perfect, you may become so wrapped up in meeting society's expectations that you fail to focus on God's expectations. To do so is a big mistake—so don't make it. Instead, focus your energies on becoming the best "you" that you can possibly be. And, when it comes to matters of conscience, seek approval not from your peers, but from your Creator.

Who will you try to please today: God or man? Your primary obligation is not to please imperfect men and women. Your obligation is to strive diligently to meet the expectations of an all-knowing and perfect God. Trust Him always. Love Him always. Praise Him always. And seek to please Him. Always.

You must never sacrifice your relationship with God
for the sake of a relationship with another person.

Charles Stanley

God is the beyond in the midst of our life.

Dietrich Bonhoeffer

PRIORITIES FOR MY LIFE

If you are burdened with a "people-pleasing" personality, outgrow
it. Realize that you can't please all of the people all of the time,
nor should you attempt to.

TIMELESS WISDOM FOR GODLY LIVING

There is a God-shaped vacuum in the heart of every man which cannot be filled by any created thing, but only by God, the Creator, made known through Jesus.

Blaise Pascal

All our offerings, whether music or martyrdom, are like the intrinsically worthless present of a child, which a father values indeed, but values only for the intention.

C. S. Lewis

Make God's will the focus of your life day by day. If you seek to please Him and Him alone, you'll find yourself satisfied with life.

Kay Arthur

My dear friends, don't let public opinion influence how you live out our glorious, Christ-originated faith.
James 2:1 MSG

It is impossible to please God doing things motivated by and produced by the flesh.

Bill Bright

MORE WORDS FROM GOD'S WORD

*Be energetic in your life of salvation, reverent and sensitive before God.
That energy is God's energy, an energy deep within you, God himself
willing and working at what will give him the most pleasure.*

Philippians 2:12-13 MSG

*By an act of faith, Enoch skipped death completely. "They looked all over
and couldn't find him because God had taken him." We know on the
basis of reliable testimony that before he was taken "he pleased God."*

Hebrews 11:5 MSG

*Everything that goes into a life of pleasing God has been miraculously
given to us by getting to know, personally and intimately, the One who
invited us to God. The best invitation we ever received!*

2 Peter 1:3 MSG

MY PRIORITIES FOR LIFE

	Check Your Priority		
	High	Med.	Low

I understand that being obedient to God means
that I cannot always please other people.

— — —

I try to associate with people who, by their actions
and their words, will encourage me to become
a better person.

— — —

I understand that it's more important to be
respected than to be liked.

— — —

The Direction of Your Thoughts

So prepare your minds for service and have self-control.

1 Peter 1:13 NCV

How will you direct your thoughts today? Will you be an upbeat believer? Will you be a man whose hopes and dreams are alive and well? Will you put a smile on your face and a song in your heart? Hopefully so. But here's a word of warning: sometimes, when pessimism, anger, or doubt threaten to hijack your emotions, you won't feel much like celebrating. That's why you must always strive to keep your thoughts headed in the right direction.

Your thoughts have the power to lift you up or drag you down; they have the power to energize you or deplete you, to inspire you to greater accomplishments or to make those accomplishments impossible.

What kind of attitude will you select today? Will you obey the words of Philippians 4:7-8 by dwelling upon those things that are "true and honorable and right?" Or will you allow yourself to be swayed by the negativity that seems to dominate our troubled world?

God intends that you experience joy and abundance, but He will not force His joy upon you; you must claim it for yourself.

It's up to you to celebrate the life that God has given you by focusing your mind upon "things that are excellent and worthy of praise." So today, spend more time thinking about your blessings and less time fretting about your hardships. Then, take time to thank the Giver of all things good for gifts that are, in truth, far too numerous to count.

It is the thoughts and intents of the heart
that shape a person's life.

John Eldredge

PRIORITIES FOR MY LIFE

Watch what you think: If your inner voice is, in reality, your inner critic, you need to tone down the criticism now. And while you're at it, train yourself to begin thinking thoughts that are more rational, more accepting, and less judgmental.
(Philippians 4:8).

TIMELESS WISDOM FOR GODLY LIVING

God's cure for evil thinking is to fill our minds with that which is good.

George Sweeting

People who do not develop and practice good thinking often find themselves at the mercy of their circumstances.

John Maxwell

Make yourselves nests of pleasant thoughts.

John Ruskin

The things we think are the things that feed our souls. If we think on pure and lovely things, we shall grow pure and lovely like them; and the converse is equally true.

Hannah Whitall Smith

Come near to God, and God will come near to you.
You sinners, clean sin out of your lives.
You who are trying to follow God and the world
at the same time, make your thinking pure.
James 4:8 NCV

The mind is like a clock that is constantly running down. It has to be wound up daily with good thoughts.

Fulton J. Sheen

MORE WORDS FROM GOD'S WORD

Dear friend, guard Clear Thinking and Common Sense with your life; don't for a minute lose sight of them. They'll keep your soul alive and well, they'll keep you fit and attractive.

Proverbs 3:21-22 MSG

I, the Lord, examine the mind, I test the heart to give to each according to his way, according to what his actions deserve.

Jeremiah 17:10 Holman CSB

May the words of my mouth and the meditation of my heart be acceptable to You, Lord, my rock and my Redeemer.

Psalm 19:14 Holman CSB

MY PRIORITIES FOR LIFE

The importance that I place on the need to direct my thoughts in the proper direction . . .

I believe that emotions are contagious, so I try to associate with people who are upbeat, optimistic, and encouraging.

I understand that when I dwell on positive thoughts, I feel better about myself and my circumstances.

Check Your Priority		
High	Med.	Low
—	—	—
—	—	—
—	—	—

Keeping Money in Perspective

For the love of money is a root of all sorts of evil,
and some by longing for it have wandered away from
the faith and pierced themselves with many griefs.

1 Timothy 6:10 NASB

Thomas Carlyle observed, "Man is a tool-using animal; without tools he is nothing, with tools he is all." Carlyle understood that mankind depends upon a wide assortment of material goods to provide ease, comfort, security, and entertainment. Our material possessions improve our lives in countless ways, but when those possessions begin to assert undo control over our daily affairs, it's time to declare "Enough stuff!"

Whenever a person becomes absorbed with the acquisition of things, complications arise. Each new acquisition costs money or time, often both. To further complicate matters, many items can be purchased, not with real money, but with the something much more insidious: debt. Debt—especially consumer debt used to purchase depreciating assets—is a modern-day form of indentured servitude.

If you're looking for a sure-fire, time-tested way to simplify your life and thereby improve your world, learn to control your possessions before they control you. Purchase only those things that make a significant contribution to your well-being and the well-being of your family. Never spend more than you make.

Understand the folly in buying consumer goods on credit. Never use credit cards as a way of financing your lifestyle.

Ask yourself this simple question: "Do I own my possessions, or do they own me?" If you don't like the answer you receive, make an iron-clad promise to stop acquiring and start divesting. As you simplify your life, you'll be amazed at the things you can do without. You be pleasantly surprised at the sense of satisfaction that accompanies your new-found moderation. And you'll understand first-hand that when it comes to material possessions, less truly is more.

How important are our material possessions? Not as important as we might think. In the lives of committed Christians, material possessions should play a rather small role. Of course, we all need the basic necessities of life, but once we meet those needs for ourselves and for our families, the piling up of possessions creates more problems than it solves. Our real riches, of course, are not of this world. We are never really rich until we are rich in spirit.

Do you find yourself wrapped up in the concerns of the material world? If so, it's time to reorder your priorities by turning your thoughts and your prayers to more important matters. And, it's time to begin storing up riches that will endure throughout eternity: the spiritual kind.

PRIORITIES FOR MY LIFE

Materialism Made Simple: The world wants you to believe that "money and stuff" can buy happiness. Don't believe it! Genuine happiness comes not from money, but from the things that money can't buy—starting, of course, with your relationship to God and His only begotten Son.

TIMELESS WISDOM FOR GODLY LIVING

Your priorities, passions, goals, and fears are shown clearly in the flow of your money.

Dave Ramsey

Servants of God are always more concerned about ministry than money.

Rick Warren

Money separates people more often than it joins them.

Liz Curtis Higgs

No man can stand in front of Jesus Christ and say "I want to make money."

Oswald Chambers

> *Do not love the world or the things in the world.*
> *If anyone loves the world,*
> *the love of the Father is not in him.*
> *1 John 2:15 NKJV*

God is entitled to a portion of our income. Not because He needs it, but because we need to give it.

James Dobson

MORE WORDS FROM GOD'S WORD

He who trusts in his riches will fall, but the righteous will flourish . . . .

Proverbs 11:28 NKJV

For what will it profit a man if he gains the whole world, and loses his own soul? Or what will a man give in exchange for his soul?

Mark 8:36-37 NKJV

The borrower is a slave to the lender.

Proverbs 22:7 Holman CSB

Based on the gift they have received, everyone should use it to serve others, as good managers of the varied grace of God.

1 Peter 4:10 Holman CSB

MY PRIORITIES FOR LIFE

Every day I will work to make certain that my possessions don't possess me.

I believe it is important to place spiritual possessions above material ones.

I believe that my enjoyment of life has less to do with material possessions and more to do with my relationships—beginning with my relationship to God.

Check Your Priority		
High	Med.	Low
—	—	—
—	—	—
—	—	—

Too Quick to Judge?

Stop judging others, and you will not be judged.
Stop criticizing others, or it will all come back on you.
If you forgive others, you will be forgiven.

Luke 6:37 NLT

Even the most devoted Christians may fall prey to a powerful yet subtle temptation: the temptation to judge others. But as believers, we are commanded to refrain from such behavior. The warning of Matthew 7:1 is clear: "Judge not, that ye be not judged" (KJV).

Are you one of those guys who finds it easy to judge others? If so, it's time to make radical changes in the way you view the world and the people who inhabit it.

When considering the shortcomings of others, you must remember this: in matters of judgement, God does not need (or want) your help. Why? Because God is perfectly capable of judging the human heart . . . while you are not. This message is made clear by the teachings of Jesus.

As Jesus came upon a young woman who had been condemned by the Pharisees, He spoke not only to the crowd that was gathered there, but also to all generations, when He warned, "He that is without sin among you, let him first cast a stone at her" (John 8:7 KJV). Christ's message is clear: because we are all sinners, we are commanded to refrain from judging others. Yet the irony is this: it is precisely because we are sinners that we are so quick to judge.

All of us have fallen short of God's laws, and none of us, therefore, are qualified to "cast the first stone." Thankfully, God has forgiven us, and we, too, must forgive others. Let us refrain, then, from judging our family members, our friends, and our loved ones. Instead, let us forgive them and love them in the same way that God has forgiven us.

An individual Christian may see fit to give up all sorts of things for special reasons—marriage, or meat, or beer, or cinema; but the moment he starts saying these things are bad in themselves, or looking down his nose at other people who do use them, he has taken the wrong turn.

C. S. Lewis

PRIORITIES FOR MY LIFE

Your ability to judge others requires a divine insight that you simply don't have. So do everybody (including yourself) a favor: don't judge.

TIMELESS WISDOM FOR GODLY LIVING

Forget the faults of others by remembering your own.

John Bunyan

Turn your attention upon yourself and beware of judging the deeds of other men, for in judging others a man labors vainly, often makes mistakes, and easily sins; whereas, in judging and taking stock of himself he does something that is always profitable.

Thomas à Kempis

Christians think they are prosecuting attorneys or judges, when, in reality, God has called all of us to be witnesses.

Warren Wiersbe

> *"Why do you look at the speck in your brother's eye, but don't notice the log in your own eye? Or how can you say to your brother, 'Let me take the speck out of your eye,' and look, there's a log in your eye? Hypocrite! First take the log out of your eye, and then you will see clearly to take the speck out of your brother's eye."*
>
> Matthew 7:3-5 Holman CSB

Don't judge other people more harshly than you want God to judge you.

Marie T. Freeman

MORE WORDS FROM GOD'S WORD

You, therefore, have no excuse, you who pass judgment on someone else, for at whatever point you judge the other, you are condemning yourself.

Romans 2:1 NIV

Speak and act as those who will be judged by the law of freedom. For judgment is without mercy to the one who hasn't shown mercy. Mercy triumphs over judgment.

James 2:12-13 Holman CSB

Do not judge, or you too will be judged. For in the same way you judge others, you will be judged, and with the measure you use, it will be measured to you.

Matthew 7:1 NIV

MY PRIORITIES FOR LIFE

I believe that the Bible warns me not to judge others, and I take that warning seriously.

When I catch myself being overly judgmental, I try to stop myself and interrupt my critical thoughts before I become angry.

I find that by being less judgmental, I can improve the quality of my life.

Check Your Priority		
High	Med.	Low
—	—	—
—	—	—
—	—	—

Doing What Needs to be Done

*For the Kingdom of God is not just fancy talk;
it is living by God's power.*

1 Corinthians 4:20 NLT

The old saying is both familiar and true: actions speak louder than words. And as believers, we must beware: our actions should always give credence to the changes that Christ can make in the lives of those who walk with Him.

God calls upon each of us to act in accordance with His will and with respect for His commandments. If we are to be responsible believers, we must realize that it is never enough to hear the instructions of God; we must also live by them. And it is never enough to wait idly by while others do God's work here on earth; we, too, must act. Doing God's work is a responsibility that each of us must bear, and when we do, our loving Heavenly Father rewards our efforts with a bountiful harvest.

Are you in the habit of doing what needs to be done when it needs to be done, or are you a dues-paying member of the Procrastinator's Club? If you've acquired the habit of doing things sooner rather than later, congratulations! But, if you find yourself putting off all those unpleasant tasks until later (or never), it's time to think about the consequences of your behavior.

One way that you can learn to defeat procrastination by paying less attention to your fears and more attention to your responsibilities. So, when you're faced with a difficult choice or an unpleasant responsibility, don't spend endless hours fretting over your fate. Simply seek God's counsel and get busy. When you do, you will be richly rewarded because of your willingness to act.

Let us not be content to wait and see what will happen, but give us the determination to make the right things happen.

Peter Marshall

PRIORITIES FOR MY LIFE

If unpleasant work needs to be done, do it sooner rather than later. It's easy to put off unpleasant tasks until "later." A far better strategy is this: Do the unpleasant work first so you can enjoy the rest of the day.

TIMELESS WISDOM FOR GODLY LIVING

We must not sit still and look for miracles; up and doing, and the Lord will be with thee. Prayer and pains, through faith in Christ Jesus, will do anything.

John Eliot

From the very moment one feels called to act is born the strength to bear whatever horror one will feel or see. In some inexplicable way, terror loses its overwhelming power when it becomes a task that must be faced.

Emmi Bonhoeffer

Start by doing what's necessary, then what's possible, and suddenly you're doing the impossible.

St. Francis of Assisi

> *Therefore, get your minds ready for action, being self-disciplined, and set your hope completely on the grace to be brought to you at the revelation of Jesus Christ.*
> 1 Peter 1:13 Holman CSB

Paul did one thing. Most of us dabble in forty things. Are you a doer or a dabbler?

Vance Havner

MORE WORDS FROM GOD'S WORD

But prove yourselves doers of the word, and not merely hearers.

James 1:22 NASB

Are there those among you who are truly wise and understanding? Then they should show it by living right and doing good things with a gentleness that comes from wisdom.

James 3:13 NCV

The prudent see danger and take refuge, but the simple keep going and suffer from it.

Proverbs 27:12 NIV

If the way you live isn't consistent with what you believe, then it's wrong.

Romans 14:23 MSG

MY PRIORITIES FOR LIFE

	Check Your Priority	
High	Med.	Low

I believe that my testimony is more powerful when actions accompany my words.

— — —

I see the hypocrisy in saying one thing and doing another, so I do my best to act in accordance with my beliefs.

— — —

When God speaks to me, I listen, and I go to work.

— — —

Living With
the Living Word

Heaven and earth will pass away, but My words will never pass away.

Matthew 24:35 Holman CSB

God's promises are found in a book like no other: the Holy Bible. The Bible is a road map for life here on earth and for life eternal. As Christians, we are called upon to trust its promises, to follow its commandments, and to share its Good News.

As believers, we must study the Bible each day and meditate upon its meaning for our lives. Otherwise, we deprive ourselves of a priceless gift from our Creator. God's Holy Word is, indeed, a transforming, life-changing, one-of-a-kind treasure. And, a passing acquaintance with the Good Book is insufficient for Christians who seek to obey God's Word and to understand His will.

God has made promises to mankind and to you. God's promises never fail and they never grow old. You must trust those promises and share them with your family, with your friends, and with the world.

Are you standing on the promises of God? Are you expecting God to do wonderful things, or are you living beneath a cloud of apprehension and doubt? The familiar words of

Psalm 118:24 remind us of a profound yet simple truth: "This is the day which the LORD hath made; we will rejoice and be glad in it" (KJV). Do you trust that promise, and do you live accordingly? If so, you are living the passionate life that God intends.

For passionate believers, every day begins and ends with God's Son and God's promises. When we accept Christ into our hearts, God promises us the opportunity for earthy peace and spiritual abundance. But more importantly, God promises us the priceless gift of eternal life.

As we face the inevitable challenges of life-here-on-earth, we must arm ourselves with the promises of God's Holy Word. When we do, we can expect the best, not only for the day ahead, but also for all eternity.

Believe God's Word and power more than you believe
your own feelings and experiences.

Samuel Rutherford

PRIORITIES FOR MY LIFE

Trust God's Word: Charles Swindoll writes, "There are four words I wish we would never forget, and they are, "God keeps His word." And remember: When it comes to studying God's Word, school is always in session.

TIMELESS WISDOM FOR GODLY LIVING

I have found in the Bible words for my inmost thoughts, songs for my joy, utterance for my hidden griefs and pleadings for my shame and feebleness.

Samuel Taylor Coleridge

To say the Bible is infallible and inerrant is to declare that Scripture is totally trustworthy. Consequently, we must approach the text humbly and expectantly, open to being taught by the Spirit.

Stanley Grenz

If we are not continually fed with God's Word, we will starve spiritually.

Stormie Omartian

But the word of the Lord endures forever.
And this is the word that was preached
as the gospel to you.
1 Peter 1:25 Holman CSB

A thorough knowledge of the Bible is worth more than a college education.

Theodore Roosevelt

MORE WORDS FROM GOD'S WORD

All Scripture is inspired by God and is profitable for teaching, for rebuking, for correcting, for training in righteousness, so that the man of God may be complete, equipped for every good work.

2 Timothy 3:16-17 Holman CSB

The one who is from God listens to God's words. This is why you don't listen, because you are not from God.

John 8:47 Holman CSB

The words of the Lord are pure words, like silver tried in a furnace . . . .

Psalm 12:6 NKJV

MY PRIORITIES FOR LIFE

I believe that "head knowledge" is important, but that "heart knowledge" is imperative.

I have found that my personal experiences have the power to transform knowledge into wisdom, so I strive to learn the lessons that my experiences can teach me.

I understand that wisdom is found in God's Word, and I seek to gain God's wisdom through daily Bible readings.

Check Your Priority		
High	Med.	Low
—	—	—
—	—	—
—	—	—

God's Perfect Love

We know how much God loves us,
and we have put our trust in him. God is love,
and all who live in love live in God, and God lives in them.

1 John 4:16 NLT

God's love for you is bigger and better than you can imagine. In fact, God's love is far too big to comprehend (in this lifetime). But this much we know: God loves you so much that He sent His Son Jesus to come to this earth and to die for you. And, when you accepted Jesus into your heart, God gave you a gift that is more precious than gold: the gift of eternal life. Now, precisely because you are a wondrous creation treasured by God, a question presents itself: What will you do in response to God's love? Will you ignore it or embrace it? Will you return it or neglect it? The decision, of course, is yours and yours alone.

When you embrace God's love, you are forever changed. When you embrace God's love, you feel differently about yourself, your neighbors, and your world. When you embrace God's love, you share His message and you obey His commandments.

When you accept the Father's gift of grace, you are blessed here on earth and throughout all eternity. So do yourself a favor right now: accept God's love with open arms and welcome

His Son Jesus into your heart. When you do, your life will be changed today, tomorrow, and forever.

God's love is measureless. It is more: it is boundless.
It has no bounds because it is not a thing but a facet of
the essential nature of God. His love is something he is,
and because he is infinite, that love can enfold
the whole created world in itself and have room for
ten thousand times ten thousand worlds beside.

A. W. Tozer

For God so loved the world, that he gave his only begotten Son,
that whosoever believeth in him should not perish,
but have everlasting life.

John 3:16 KJV

PRIORITIES FOR MY LIFE

Remember: God's love for you is too big to understand with your brain . . . but it's not too big to feel with your heart.

TIMELESS WISDOM FOR GODLY LIVING

As God's children, we are the recipients of lavish love—a love that motivates us to keep trusting even when we have no idea what God is doing.

Beth Moore

God proved his love on the cross. When Christ hung, and bled, and died it was God saying to the world—I love you.

Billy Graham

After ten thousand insults, he still loves you as infinitely as ever.

C. H. Spurgeon

There is no pit so deep that God's love is not deeper still.

Corrie ten Boom

As the Father loved Me,
I also have loved you; abide in My love.
John 15:9 NKJV

The life of faith is a daily exploration of the constant and countless ways in which God's grace and love are experienced.

Eugene Peterson

MORE WORDS FROM GOD'S WORD

The unfailing love of the LORD never ends! By his mercies we have been kept from complete destruction.

Lamentations 3:22 NLT

His banner over me was love.

Song of Solomon 2:4 KJV

Unfailing love surrounds those who trust the LORD.

Psalm 32:10 NLT

For the LORD your God has arrived to live among you. He is a mighty Savior. He will rejoice over you with great gladness. With his love, he will calm all your fears. He will exult over you by singing a happy song.

Zephaniah 3:17 NLT

MY PRIORITIES FOR LIFE

	Check Your Priority	
High	Med.	Low

I believe God loves me.

— — —

I believe God wants me to love Him in return.

— — —

I believe that the more I worship God, the more that I study His Word, and the more time that I spend quietly with Him, the more I will sense His presence and His love.

— — —

The Power of Perseverance

*Let us not become weary in doing good, for at the proper time
we will reap a harvest if we do not give up.*

Galatians 6:9 NIV

As you continue to seek God's purpose for your life,
you will undoubtedly experience your fair share of
disappointments, detours, false starts, and failures.
When you do, don't become discouraged: God's not finished
with you yet.

The old saying is as true today as it was when it was first
spoken: "Life is a marathon, not a sprint." That's why wise
travelers (like you) select a traveling companion who never tires
and never falters. That partner, of course, is your Heavenly
Father.

The next time you find your courage tested to the limit,
remember that God is as near as your next breath, and remember
that He offers strength and comfort to His children. He is your
shield and your strength; He is your protector and your deliverer.
Call upon Him in your hour of need and then be comforted.
Whatever your challenge, whatever your trouble, God can help
you persevere. And that's precisely what He'll do if you ask Him.

Perhaps you are in a hurry for God to help you resolve your difficulties. Perhaps you're anxious to earn the rewards that you feel you've already earned from life. Perhaps you're drumming your fingers, impatiently waiting for God to act. If so, be forewarned: God operates on His own timetable, not yours. Sometimes, God may answer your prayers with silence, and when He does, you must patiently persevere. In times of trouble, you must remain steadfast and trust in the merciful goodness of your Heavenly Father. Whatever your problem, He can handle it. Your job is to keep persevering until He does.

Keep adding, keep walking, keep advancing; do not stop, do not turn back, do not turn from the straight road.

St. Augustine

PRIORITIES FOR MY LIFE

Feeling tired, troubled, and discouraged? Maybe you're not getting enough sleep. Do you get a full eight hours of sleep each night? You should. To be sufficiently strong tomorrow, you need sufficient sleep tonight.

TIMELESS WISDOM FOR GODLY LIVING

Let us not cease to do the utmost, that we may incessantly go forward in the way of the Lord; and let us not despair of the smallness of our accomplishments.

John Calvin

Your life is not a boring stretch of highway. It's a straight line to heaven. And just look at the fields ripening along the way. Look at the tenacity and endurance. Look at the grains of righteousness. You'll have quite a crop at harvest . . . so don't give up!

Joni Eareckson Tada

In the Bible, patience is not a passive acceptance of circumstances. It is a courageous perseverance in the face of suffering and difficulty.

Warren Wiersbe

For you have need of endurance, so that when you have done the will of God, you may receive what was promised.
Hebrews 10:36 NASB

Battles are won in the trenches, in the grit and grime of courageous determination; they are won day by day in the arena of life.

Charles Swindoll

MORE WORDS FROM GOD'S WORD

Thanks be to God! He gives us the victory through our Lord Jesus Christ. Therefore, my dear brothers, stand firm. Let nothing move you. Always give yourselves fully to the work of the Lord, because you know that your labor in the Lord is not in vain.

1 Corinthians 15:57-58 NIV

Be diligent that ye may be found of him in peace, without spot, and blameless.

2 Peter 3:14 KJV

I do not consider myself yet to have taken hold of it. But one thing I do: Forgetting what is behind and straining toward what is ahead, I press on toward the goal to win the prize for which God has called me heavenward in Christ Jesus.

Philippians 3:13-14 NIV

MY PRIORITIES FOR LIFE

	Check Your Priority	
High	Med.	Low

I have respect for the power of perseverance.

— — —

When I am discouraged, I ask God to give me strength.

— — —

For me, it is helpful to associate with people who encourage me to be courageous, optimistic, energetic, and persistent.

— — —

At Home in God's Church

For we are God's fellow workers;
you are God's field, you are God's building.

1 Corinthians 3:9 NKJV

In the Book of Acts, Luke reminds us to "feed the church of God" (20:28). As Christians who have been saved by a loving, compassionate Creator, we are compelled not only to worship Him in our hearts but also to worship Him in the presence of fellow believers.

We live in a world that is teeming with temptations and distractions—a world where good and evil struggle in a constant battle to win our hearts and souls. Our challenge, of course, is to ensure that we cast our lot on the side of God. One way to ensure that we do so is by the practice of regular, purposeful worship with our families. When we worship God faithfully and fervently, we are blessed. When we fail to worship God, we forfeit the spiritual gifts that He intends for us.

The church belongs to God; it is His just as certainly as we are His. When we help build God's church, we bear witness to the changes that He has made in our lives.

Today and every day, let us worship God with grateful hearts and helping hands as we support the church that He has created.

Let us witness to our friends, to our families, and to the world.
When we do so, we bless others—and we are blessed by the One
who sent His Son to die so that we might have eternal life.

The Church's one foundation is Jesus Christ, her Lord;
She is His new creation by water and the Word.

Samuel J. Stone

It has always been the work of the church to
bring others to belief in Christ and to experience
a personal relationship with Him.

Charles Stanley

PRIORITIES FOR MY LIFE

Make church a celebration, not an obligation: Your attitude
towards church is important, in part, because it is contagious . . .
so celebrate accordingly!

TIMELESS WISDOM FOR GODLY LIVING

To model the kingdom of God in the world, the church must not only be a repentant community, committed to truth, but also a holy community.

Chuck Colson

What the church needs is not better machinery nor new organizations, but instead it needs men whom the Holy Spirit can use—men of prayer, men mighty in prayer.

E. M. Bounds

Every time a new person comes to God, every time someone's gifts find expression in the fellowship of believers, every time a family in need is surrounded by the caring church, the truth is affirmed anew: the Church triumphant is alive and well!

Gloria Gaither

Don't you realize that all of you together are the temple of God and that the Spirit of God lives in you?
1 Corinthians 3:16 NLT

The church is where it's at. The first place of Christian service for any Christian is in a local church.

Jerry Clower

MORE WORDS FROM GOD'S WORD

Now you are the body of Christ, and members individually.

1 Corinthians 12:27 NKJV

Be on guard for yourselves and for all the flock, among which the Holy Spirit has made you overseers, to shepherd the church of God which He purchased with His own blood.

Acts 20:28 NASB

The church, you see, is not peripheral to the world; the world is peripheral to the church. The church is Christ's body, in which he speaks and acts, by which he fills everything with his presence.

Ephesians 1:23 MSG

Then He began to teach them: "Is it not written, My house will be called a house of prayer for all nations? But you have made it a den of thieves!"

Mark 11:17 Holman CSB

MY PRIORITIES FOR LIFE

	Check Your Priority	
High	Med.	Low

I understand the need to worship God in church.

— — —

I attend church because I need to give and to learn.

— — —

I understand the need to be an active member
of my church.

— — —

Beyond Busyness

Don't burn out; keep yourselves fueled and aflame.
Be alert servants of the Master, cheerfully expectant.
Don't quit in hard times; pray all the harder.

Romans 12:11-12 MSG

Has the busy pace of life robbed you of the peace that might otherwise be yours through Jesus Christ? If so, you are simply too busy for your own good. Through His only begotten Son, God offers you a peace that passes human understanding, but He won't force His peace upon you; in order to experience it, you must slow down long enough to sense His presence and His love.

Time is a nonrenewable gift from God. How will you use it? You know from experience that you should invest some time each day in yourself, but finding time to do so is easier said than done. As a busy Christian, you may have difficulty investing large blocks of time in much-needed thought and self-reflection. If so, it may be time to reorder your priorities.

"First things first" is an adage that's easy to speak but hard to put into practice. Why? Because we live in a demanding world, a world filled with many distractions. And as we try to prioritize our days and our lives, we are confronted by so many people who are expecting so many things from us! But we must never allow ourselves to become so busy that we fail to make time for God.

God has big plans for you. Discovering those plans will require trial and error, meditation and prayer, faith and perseverance. The moments of silence that you claim for yourself will help you gather your thoughts and sense direction from your Creator.

Each waking moment holds the potential to think a creative thought or offer a heartfelt prayer. So even if you're a person with too many demands and too few hours in which to meet them, don't panic. Instead, be comforted in the knowledge that when you sincerely seek to discover God's priorities for your life, He will provide answers in marvelous and surprising ways.

Remember: this is the day that God has made and that He has filled it with countless opportunities to love, to serve, and to seek His guidance. Seize those opportunities today, and keep seizing them every day that you live. And as a gift to yourself, to your family, and to the world, slow down and claim the inner peace that is your spiritual birthright: the peace of Jesus Christ. It is offered freely; it has been paid for in full; it is yours for the asking. So ask. And then share.

PRIORITIES FOR MY LIFE

Keep it simple. Max Lucado writes, "The most powerful life is the most simple life. The most powerful life is the life that knows where it's going, that knows where the source of strength is; it is the life that stays free of clutter and happenstance and hurriedness." He's right you know.

TIMELESS WISDOM FOR GODLY LIVING

It is common to think that activity in the service of Christ is the indication of the blessing of God, but be aware of barrenness in a busy life.

Franklin Graham

Much of what is sacred is hidden in the ordinary, everyday moments of our lives. To see something of the sacred in those moments takes slowing down so we can live our lives more reflectively.

Ken Gire

Busyness is the great enemy of relationships.

Rick Warren

Careful planning puts you ahead in the long run; hurry and scurry puts you further behind.
Proverbs 21:5 MSG

Some of us would do more for the Lord if we did less.

Vance Havner

The demand of every day kept me so busy that I subconsciously equated my busyness with commitment to Christ.

Vonette Bright

MORE WORDS FROM GOD'S WORD

You can't go wrong when you love others. When you add up everything in the law code, the sum total is love. But make sure that you don't get so absorbed and exhausted in taking care of all your day-by-day obligations that you lose track of the time and doze off, oblivious to God.

Romans 13:10-11 MSG

Jesus said, "You're tied down to the mundane; I'm in touch with what is beyond your horizons. You live in terms of what you see and touch. I'm living on other terms. I told you that you were missing God in all this. You're at a dead end. If you won't believe I am who I say I am, you're at the dead end of sins. You're missing God in your lives."

John 8:23-24 MSG

I said to myself, "Relax and rest. God has showered you with blessings."

Psalm 116:7 MSG

MY PRIORITIES FOR LIFE

	Check Your Priority	
High	Med.	Low

I understand the importance of setting priorities.

— — —

After I have established priorities for the coming day, I value the importance of doing first things first.

— — —

Because I understand that I cannot do everything, I understand the importance of saying no when it's appropriate to do so.

— — —

Acceptance for Today

Shall I not drink from the cup the Father has given me?

John 18:11 NLT

If you're like most men, you like being in control. Period. You want things to happen according to your wishes and according to your timetable. But sometimes, God has other plans . . . and He always has the final word.

The American Theologian Reinhold Niebuhr composed a profoundly simple verse that came to be known as the Serenity Prayer: "God, grant me the serenity to accept the things I cannot change, the courage to change the things I can, and the wisdom to know the difference." Niebuhr's words are far easier to recite than they are to live by.

Oswald Chambers correctly observed, "Our Lord never asks us to decide for Him; He asks us to yield to Him—a very different matter." These words remind us that even when we cannot understand the workings of God, we must trust Him and accept His will.

All of us experience adversity and pain. As human beings with limited comprehension, we can never fully understand the will of our Father in Heaven. But as believers in a benevolent God, we must always trust His providence.

When Jesus went to the Mount of Olives, as described in Luke 22, He poured out His heart to God. Jesus knew of the agony that He was destined to endure, but He also knew that God's will must be done. We, like our Savior, face trials that bring fear and trembling to the very depths of our souls, but like Christ, we too must ultimately seek God's will, not our own.

Are you embittered by a personal tragedy that you did not deserve and cannot understand? If so, it's time to make peace with life. It's time to forgive others, and, if necessary, to forgive yourself. It's time to accept the unchangeable past, to embrace the priceless present, and to have faith in the promise of tomorrow. It's time to trust God completely. And it's time to reclaim the peace—His peace—that can and should be yours.

So if you've encountered unfortunate circumstances that are beyond your power to control, accept those circumstances . . . and trust God. When you do, you can be comforted in the knowledge that your Creator is both loving and wise, and that He understands His plans perfectly, even when you do not.

I am truly grateful that faith enables me to move past the question of "Why?"

Zig Ziglar

PRIORITIES FOR MY LIFE

It is easier to trust God when times are good and more difficult to trust Him when times are difficult. Our challenge, as believers, is to trust God in every situation.

TIMELESS WISDOM FOR GODLY LIVING

Have courage for the great sorrows of life and patience for the small ones; and when you have laboriously accomplished your daily task, go to sleep in peace. God is awake.

Victor Hugo

What cannot be altered must be borne, not blamed.

Thomas Fuller

The key to contentment is to consider. Consider who you are and be satisfied with that. Consider what you have and be satisfied with that. Consider what God's doing and be satisfied with that.

Luci Swindoll

He is the Lord. Let him do what he thinks is best.
1 Samuel 3:18 NCV

The more comfortable we are with mystery in our journey, the more rest we will know along the way.

John Eldredge

MORE WORDS FROM GOD'S WORD

The Lord says, "Forget what happened before, and do not think about the past. Look at the new thing I am going to do. It is already happening. Don't you see it? I will make a road in the desert and rivers in the dry land."

Isaiah 43:18-19 NCV

He said, "I came naked from my mother's womb, and I will be stripped of everything when I die. The LORD gave me everything I had, and the LORD has taken it away. Praise the name of the LORD!"

Job 1:21 NLT

For everything created by God is good, and nothing should be rejected if it is received with thanksgiving.

1 Timothy 4:4 Holman CSB

MY PRIORITIES FOR LIFE

	Check Your Priority		
	High	Med.	Low

I believe that it is important to trust God even
when I don't understand why certain things happen. — — —

I think it is important to learn from the past,
to accept the past, and to live in the present. — — —

I think it is important to change what I need to
change and accept that which I can't change. — — —

Asking
and Accepting

*If you need wisdom—if you want to know what God wants you to do—
ask him, and he will gladly tell you. He will not resent your asking.*

James 1:5 NLT

How often do you ask God for His help and His wisdom?
Occasionally? Intermittently? Whenever you experience
a crisis? Hopefully not. Hopefully, you've acquired
the habit of asking for God's assistance early and often. And
hopefully, you have learned to seek His guidance in every aspect
of your life.

Jesus made it clear to His disciples: they should petition
God to meet their needs. So should you. Genuine, heartfelt
prayer produces powerful changes in you and in your world.
When you lift your heart to God, you open yourself to a never-
ending source of divine wisdom and infinite love.

James 5:16 makes a promise that God intends to keep: when
you pray earnestly, fervently, and often, great things will happen.
Too many people, however, are too timid or too pessimistic to ask
God to do big things. Please don't count yourself among their
number.

God can do great things through you if you have the
courage to ask Him (and the determination to keep asking Him).

But don't expect Him to do all the work. When you do your part, He will do His part—and when He does, you can expect miracles to happen.

The Bible promises that God will guide you if you let Him. Your job is to let Him. But sometimes, you will be tempted to do otherwise. Sometimes, you'll be tempted to go along with the crowd; other times, you'll be tempted to do things your way, not God's way. When you feel those temptations, resist them.

God has promised that when you ask for His help, He will not withhold it. So ask. Ask Him to meet the needs of your day. Ask Him to lead you, to protect you, and to correct you. Then, trust the answers He gives.

God stands at the door and waits. When you knock, He opens. When you ask, He answers. Your task, of course, is to make God a full partner in every aspect of your life—and to seek His guidance prayerfully, confidently, and often.

All we have to do is to acknowledge our need,
move from self-sufficiency to dependence,
and ask God to become our hiding place.

Bill Hybels

PRIORITIES FOR MY LIFE

Pray early and often. One way to make sure that your heart is in tune with God is to pray often. The more you talk to God, the more He will talk to you.

TIMELESS WISDOM FOR GODLY LIVING

Some people think God does not like to be troubled with our constant asking. But, the way to trouble God is not to come at all.

D. L. Moody

Notice that we must ask. And we will sometimes struggle to hear and struggle with what we hear. But personally, it's worth it. I'm after the path of life—and he alone knows it.

John Eldredge

Don't be afraid to ask your heavenly Father for anything you need. Indeed, nothing is too small for God's attention or too great for his power.

Dennis Swanberg

From now on, whatever you request along the lines of who I am and what I am doing, I'll do it. That's how the Father will be seen for who he is in the Son. I mean it. Whatever you request in this way, I'll do.

John 14:13-14 MSG

When will we realize that we're not troubling God with our questions and concerns? His heart is open to hear us—his touch nearer than our next thought—as if no one in the world existed but us. Our very personal God wants to hear from us personally.

Gigi Graham Tchividjian

MORE WORDS FROM GOD'S WORD

You did not choose me, but I chose you and appointed you to go and bear fruit—fruit that will last. Then the Father will give you whatever you ask in my name.

John 15:16 NIV

Until now you have not asked for anything in my name. Ask and you will receive, so that your joy will be the fullest possible joy.

John 16:24 NCV

Do not worry about anything, but pray and ask God for everything you need, always giving thanks.

Philippians 4:6 NCV

You do not have, because you do not ask God.

James 4:2 NIV

MY PRIORITIES FOR LIFE

I understand the importance of talking to God each day.

I understand the importance of spending quiet time listening to God.

I understand the importance of making God a partner in every aspect of my life.

Check Your Priority		
High	Med.	Low
—	—	—
—	—	—
—	—	—

Trusting Your Conscience

So I strive always to keep my conscience clear before God and man.

Acts 24:16 NIV

It has been said that character is what we are when nobody is watching. How true. When we do things that we know aren't right, we try to hide them from our families and friends. But even then, God is watching.

Few things in life torment us more than a guilty conscience. And, few things in life provide more contentment than the knowledge that we are obeying God's commandments. A clear conscience is one of the rewards we earn when we obey God's Word and follow His will. When we follow God's will and accept His gift of salvation, our earthly rewards are never-ceasing, and our heavenly rewards are everlasting.

Billy Graham correctly observed, "Most of us follow our conscience as we follow a wheelbarrow. We push it in front of us in the direction we want to go." If that describes you, then here's a word of warning: both you and your wheelbarrow are headed for trouble.

Do you place a high value on the need to keep your conscience clear? If so, keep up the good work. But if you're tempted to do something that you'd rather the world not know about, remember this: You can sometimes keep secrets from other people, but you can never keep secrets from God. God knows what you think and what you do. And if you want to please Him, you must start with good intentions, a pure heart, and a clear conscience.

If you sincerely wish to honor your Father in heaven, follow His commandments. When you do, your character will take care of itself . . . and so will your conscience. Then, as you journey through life, you won't need to look over your shoulder to see who—besides God—is watching.

One's conscience can only be satisfied when God is satisfied.

C. H. Spurgeon

PRIORITIES FOR MY LIFE

Listening to that little voice . . . That quiet little voice inside your head will guide you down the right path if you listen carefully. Very often, your conscience will actually tell you what God wants you to do. So listen, learn, and behave accordingly.

TIMELESS WISDOM FOR GODLY LIVING

Your conscience is your alarm system. It's your protection.

Charles Stanley

My conscience is captive to the word of God.

Martin Luther

The convicting work of the Holy Spirit awakens, disturbs, and judges.

Franklin Graham

There is no pillow so soft as a clear conscience.

French Proverb

*If then you were raised with Christ,
seek those things which are above, where Christ is,
sitting at the right hand of God.
Set your mind on things above,
not on things on the earth.*

Colossians 3:1-2 NKJV

A good conscience is a continual feast.

Francis Bacon

MORE WORDS FROM GOD'S WORD

Let us come near to God with a sincere heart and a sure faith, because we have been made free from a guilty conscience, and our bodies have been washed with pure water.

Hebrews 10:22 NCV

I will maintain my righteousness and never let go of it; my conscience will not reproach me as long as I live.

Job 27:6 NIV

For indeed, the kingdom of God is within you.

Luke 17:21 NKJV

Do not conform any longer to the pattern of this world, but be transformed by the renewing of your mind. Then you will be able to test and approve what God's will is—his good, pleasing and perfect will.

Romans 12:2 NIV

MY PRIORITIES FOR LIFE

Check Your Priority

High   Med.   Low

I understand the value of a clear conscience.

—   —   —

I believe that it is important that I attune my thoughts to God's will for my life.

—   —   —

When I prepare to make an important decision, I listen to my conscience very carefully.

—   —   —

Beyond Doubt

If you don't know what you're doing, pray to the Father.
He loves to help. You'll get his help, and won't be condescended
to when you ask for it. Ask boldly, believingly, without a second thought.
People who "worry their prayers" are like wind-whipped waves.
Don't think you're going to get anything from the Master that way,
adrift at sea, keeping all your options open.

James 1:5-8 MSG

Doubts come in several shapes and sizes: doubts about God, doubts about the future, and doubts about your own abilities, for starters. And what, precisely, does God's Word say in response to these doubts? The Bible is clear: when we are beset by doubts, of whatever kind, we must draw ourselves nearer to God through worship and through prayer. When we do so, God, the loving Father who has never left our sides, draws ever closer to us (James 4:8).

In the book of Matthew, we are told of a terrible storm that rose quickly on the Sea of Galilee while Jesus and His disciples were in a boat, far from shore. The disciples were filled with fear. Although they had witnessed many miracles firsthand—although they had walked and talked with Him—the disciples were still filled with doubts. So they cried out to their Master, and Christ responded, "Why are you fearful, O you of little faith?" Then He arose and rebuked the winds and the sea, and there was a great calm. So the men marveled, saying, "Who can this be, that even the winds and the sea obey Him?" (Matthew 8:26-27 NKJV).

Sometimes, like Jesus' disciples, we feel threatened by the storms of life. Sometimes we may feel distant from God; sometimes we may question His power or His plans. During these moments, when we our hearts are flooded with uncertainty, we must remember that God is not simply near, He is here.

Have you ever felt your faith in God slipping away? If so, you are not alone. Every life—including yours—is a series of successes and failures, celebrations and disappointments, joys and sorrows, hopes and doubts. Even the most faithful Christians are overcome by occasional bouts of fear and doubt, and so, too, will you. But even when you feel far removed from God, God never leaves your side, not for an instant. He is always with you, always willing to calm the storms of life. When you sincerely seek His presence—and when you genuinely seek to establish a deeper, more meaningful relationship with His Son—God is prepared to touch your heart, to calm your fears, to answer your doubts, and to restore your soul.

Seldom do you enjoy the luxury of making decisions that are based on enough evidence to absolutely silence all skepticism.

Bill Hybels

PRIORITIES FOR MY LIFE

Doubts Creeping In? Increase the amount of time you spend in Bible study, prayer, and worship.

TIMELESS WISDOM FOR GODLY LIVING

In our constant struggle to believe, we are likely to overlook the simple fact that a bit of healthy disbelief is sometimes as needful as faith to the welfare of our souls.

A. W. Tozer

We basically have two choices to make in dealing with the mysteries of God. We can wrestle with Him or we can rest in Him.

Calvin Miller

I was learning something important: we are most vulnerable to the piercing winds of doubt when we distance ourselves from the mission and fellowship to which Christ has called us. Our night of discouragement will seem endless and our task impossible, unless we recognize that He stands in our midst.

Joni Eareckson Tada

> *Purify your hearts, ye double-minded.*
> James 4:8 KJV

There is a difference between doubt and unbelief. Doubt is a matter of mind: we cannot understand what God is doing or why He is doing it. Unbelief is a matter of will: we refuse to believe God's Word and obey what He tells us to do.

Warren Wiersbe

MORE WORDS FROM GOD'S WORD

Immediately the father of the child cried out and said with tears, "Lord, I believe; help my unbelief!"

Mark 9:24 NKJV

So He said, "Come." And when Peter had come down out of the boat, he walked on the water to go to Jesus. But when he saw that the wind was boisterous, he was afraid; and beginning to sink he cried out, saying, "Lord, save me!" And immediately Jesus stretched out His hand and caught him, and said to him, "O you of little faith, why did you doubt?" And when they got into the boat, the wind ceased.

Matthew 14:29-32 NKJV

Jesus said, "Because you have seen Me, you have believed. Blessed are those who believe without seeing."

John 20:29 Holman CSB

MY PRIORITIES FOR LIFE

	Check Your Priority		
	High	Med.	Low
Even when I cannot understand why certain things happen, I trust God's plan for my life and the world.	—	—	—
When I have doubts, I believe that it is important to take those doubts to the Lord.	—	—	—
I do not believe because I see and understand; I see and understand because I believe.	—	—	—

Living Courageously

Be strong and courageous, and do the work.
Don't be afraid or discouraged by the size of the task,
for the LORD God, my God, is with you.
He will not fail you or forsake you.

1 Chronicles 28:20 NLT

To his adoring fans, he was the "Sultan of Swat." He was Babe Ruth, the one-of-a-kind baseball legend who set records for both home runs and strikeouts. Babe's philosophy was simple. He said, "Never let the fear of striking out get in your way." That's smart advice on the diamond or off.

Of course it's never wise to take foolish risks (so buckle up, slow down, and don't do anything stupid!). But when it comes to the game of life, you should not let the fear of failure keep you from taking your swings.

As we consider the uncertainties of the future, we are confronted with a powerful temptation: the temptation to "play it safe." Unwilling to move mountains, we fret over molehills. Unwilling to entertain great hopes for the tomorrow, we focus on the unfairness of the today. Unwilling to trust God completely, we take timid half-steps when God intends that we make giant leaps. Why are we willing to settle for baby steps when God wants us to leap tall buildings in a single bound? Because we are fearful that we might fail.

The occasional disappointments and failures of life are inevitable. Such setbacks are simply the price that we must occasionally pay for our willingness to take risks as we follow our dreams. But even when we encounter bitter disappointments, we must never lose faith. And we must remember that in the game of life, we never hit a home run unless we are willing to step up to the plate and swing.

Today, ask God for the courage to step beyond the boundaries of your self-doubts. Ask Him to guide you to a place where you can realize your full potential—a place where you are freed from the fear of failure. Ask Him to do His part, and promise Him that you will do your part. Don't ask Him to lead you to a "safe" place; ask Him to lead you to the "right" place . . . and remember: those two places are seldom the same.

Courage is almost a contradiction in terms.
It means a strong desire to live taking the form
of a readiness to die.

G. K. Chesterton

PRIORITIES FOR MY LIFE

Are you feeling anxious or fearful? If so, trust God to handle those problems that are simply too big for you to solve. Entrust the future—your future—to God.

TIMELESS WISDOM FOR GODLY LIVING

God did away with all my fear. It was time for someone to stand up—or in my case, sit down. So I refused to move.

Rosa Parks

Jesus Christ can make the weakest man into a divine dreadnought, fearing nothing.

Oswald Chambers

A man who is intimate with God will never be intimidated by men.

Leonard Ravenhill

There comes a time when we simply have to face the challenges in our lives and stop backing down.

John Eldredge

Therefore, being always of good courage . . .
we walk by faith, not by sight.
2 Corinthians 5:6-7 NASB

When once we are assured that God is good, then there can be nothing left to fear.

Hannah Whitall Smith

MORE WORDS FROM GOD'S WORD

The LORD himself goes before you and will be with you; he will never leave you nor forsake you. Do not be afraid; do not be discouraged.

Deuteronomy 31:8 NIV

So do not fear, for I am with you; do not be dismayed, for I am your God. I will strengthen you and help you; I will uphold you with my righteous right hand.

Isaiah 41:10 NIV

Peace I leave with you, my peace I give unto you: not as the world giveth, give I unto you. Let not your heart be troubled, neither let it be afraid.

John 14:27 KJV

MY PRIORITIES FOR LIFE

	Check Your Priority	
High	Med.	Low

I consider God to be my partner in every aspect of my life.

— — —

I will work diligently to resolve the challenges that concern me.

— — —

I will trust God to handle the problems that are simply too big for me to solve.

— — —

I will entrust the future—and my future—to God.

— — —

Value-based Decisions

Depend on the Lord and his strength;
always go to him for help. Remember the miracles he has done;
remember his wonders and his decisions.

Psalm 105:4-5 NCV

Life is a series of choices. Some decisions are easy to make because the consequences of those decisions are small. When the person behind the counter asks, "Want fries with that?" the necessary response requires little thought because the consequences of that decision are minor.

Some decisions, on the other hand, are big . . . very big. The biggest decision, of course, is one that far too many people ignore: the decision concerning God's only begotten Son. But if you're a believer in Christ, you've already made that choice, and you have received God's gift of grace. Perhaps now you're asking yourself "What's next, Lord?" If so, you may be facing a series of big decisions concerning your life and your future. Here are some things you can do:

1. Gather as much information as you can: don't expect to get all the facts—that's impossible—but get as many facts as you can in a reasonable amount of time. (Proverbs 24:3-4)
2. Don't be too impulsive: If you have time to make a decision, use that time to make a good decision. (Proverbs 19:2)

3. Rely on the advice of trusted friends and mentors. Proverbs 1:5 makes it clear: "A wise man will hear and increase learning, and a man of understanding will attain wise counsel." (NKJV)

4. Pray for guidance. When you seek it, He will give it. (Luke 11:9)

5. Make choices based upon values, not convenience: Trust the quiet inner voice of your conscience: Treat your conscience as you would a trusted advisor. (Luke 17:21)

6. When the time for action arrives, act. Procrastination is the enemy of progress; don't let it defeat you. (James 1:22).

As we trust God to give us wisdom for today's decisions,
He will lead us a step at a time into what
He wants us to be doing in the future.

Theodore Epp

PRIORITIES FOR MY LIFE

Slow Down! If you're about to make an important decision, don't be impulsive. Remember: big decisions have big consequences, and if you don't think about those consequences now, you may pay a big price later.

TIMELESS WISDOM FOR GODLY LIVING

Very few things motivate us to give God our undivided attention like being faced with the negative consequences of our decisions.

Charles Stanley

The location of your affections will drive the direction of your decisions.

Lisa Bevere

God always gives His best to those who leave the choice with Him.

Jim Elliot

It is the nature and the advantage of strong people that they can bring out the crucial questions and form a clear opinion about them. The weak always have to decide between alternatives that are not their own.

Dietrich Bonhoeffer

Ignorant zeal is worthless; haste makes waste.
Proverbs 19:2 MSG

Successful people make right decisions early and manage those decisions daily.

John Maxwell

MORE WORDS FROM GOD'S WORD

But Daniel purposed in his heart that he would not defile himself . . . .

Daniel 1:8 KJV

I am offering you life or death, blessings or curses. Now, choose life! . . . To choose life is to love the Lord your God, obey him, and stay close to him.

Deuteronomy 30:19-20 NCV

The thing you should want most is God's kingdom and doing what God wants. Then all these other things you need will be given to you.

Matthew 6:33 NCV

MY PRIORITIES FOR LIFE

I understand that I am accountable for the decisions I make.

In making important decisions, I understand the importance of seeking God's guidance.

I understand the importance of making decisions based upon the teachings of God's Word.

Check Your Priority		
High	Med.	Low
—	—	—
—	—	—
—	—	—

A Healthy Lifestyle

Therefore, brothers, by the mercies of God,
I urge you to present your bodies as a living sacrifice,
holy and pleasing to God; this is your spiritual worship.

Romans 12:1 Holman CSB

In the Book of Romans, Paul encourages us to make our bodies "holy and pleasing to God." Paul adds that to do so is a "spiritual act of worship." For believers, the implication is clear: God intends that we take special care of the bodies He has given us. But it's tempting to do otherwise.

We live in a fast-food world where unhealthy choices are convenient, inexpensive, and tempting. And, we live in a digital world filled with modern conveniences that often rob us of the physical exercise needed to maintain healthy lifestyles. As a result, too many of us find ourselves glued to the television, with a snack in one hand and a clicker in the other. The results are as unfortunate as they are predictable.

As adults, each of us bears a personal responsibility for the general state of our own physical health. Certainly, various aspects of health are beyond our control: illness sometimes strikes even the healthiest men and women. But for most of us, physical health is a choice: it is the result of hundreds of small decisions that we make every day of our lives. If we make decisions that promote good health, our bodies respond. But if we fall into bad habits and undisciplined lifestyles, we suffer tragic consequences.

When our unhealthy habits lead to poor health, we find it all too easy to look beyond ourselves and assign blame. In fact, we live in a society where blame has become a national obsession: we blame cigarette manufacturers, restaurants, and food producers, to name only a few. But to blame others is to miss the point: we, and we alone, are responsible for the way that we treat our bodies. And the sooner that we accept that responsibility, the sooner we can assert control over our bodies and our lives.

Do you sincerely desire to improve your physical health? If so, start by taking personal responsibility for the body that God has given you. Then, make the solemn pledge to yourself that you will begin to make the changes that are required to enjoy a longer, healthier, happier life. No one can make those changes for you; you must make them for yourself. And with God's help, you can . . . and you will.

PRIORITIES FOR MY LIFE

As you petition God each morning, ask Him for the strength and the wisdom to treat your body as His creation and His "temple." During the day ahead, you will face countless temptations to do otherwise, but with God's help, you can treat your body as the priceless, one-of-a-kind gift that it most certainly is.

TIMELESS WISDOM FOR GODLY LIVING

Our minds have been endowed with an incredible ability to affect the functioning and overall health of our bodies.

Dr. Kenneth Cooper

The only way to keep your health is to eat what you don't want, drink what you don't like, and do what you'd rather not.

Mark Twain

Our primary motivation should not be for more energy or to avoid a heart attack but to please God with our bodies.

Carole Lewis

Laughter is jogging for the insides. It increases heart rate and circulation, stimulates the immune system, and improves the muscle tone of the abdomen.

Barbara Johnson

A cheerful disposition is good for your health;
gloom and doom leave you bone-tired.
Proverbs 17:22 MSG

Exercise promotes the psychological benefits of looking and feeling healthy, and it reduces stress and stress-induced eating.

Dr. Richard Couey

MORE WORDS FROM GOD'S WORD

They brought unto him all sick people that were taken with diverse diseases and torments...and he healed them.

Matthew 4:24 KJV

Is any among you afflicted? Let him pray.

James 5:13 KJV

Beloved, I pray that in all respects you may prosper and be in good health, just as your soul prospers.

3 John 1:2 NASB

For we know that if our earthly house, a tent, is destroyed, we have a building from God, a house not made with hands, eternal in the heavens.

2 Corinthians 5:1 Holman CSB

MY PRIORITIES FOR LIFE

	Check Your Priority	
High	Med.	Low

I will consider my lifestyle a form of worship.

—	—	—

I will avail myself of the advice and counsel of my personal physician.

—	—	—

I will strive to make healthy choices today, not tomorrow.

—	—	—

Integrity Matters

Till I die, I will not deny my integrity.
I will maintain my righteousness and never let go of it;
my conscience will not reproach me as long as I live.

Job 27:5-6 NIV

Charles Swindoll correctly observed, "Nothing speaks louder or more powerfully than a life of integrity." Godly men and women agree.

Integrity is built slowly over a lifetime. It is the sum of every right decision and every honest word. It is forged on the anvil of honorable work and polished by the twin virtues of honesty and fairness. Integrity is a precious thing—difficult to build but easy to tear down.

As believers in Christ, we must seek to live each day with discipline, honesty, and faith. When we do, at least two things happen: integrity becomes a habit, and God blesses us because of our obedience to Him.

Living a life of integrity isn't always the easiest way, but it is always the right way. God clearly intends that it should be our way, too.

Oswald Chambers, the author of the Christian classic devotional text, *My Utmost For His Highest*, advised, "Never support an experience which does not have God as its source, and faith in God as its result." These words serve as a powerful reminder that, as Christians, we are called to walk with God and obey His commandments. But, we live in a world that presents us with countless temptations to stray far from God's path. We Christians, when confronted with sins of any kind, have clear instructions: Walk—or better yet run—in the opposite direction.

It has been said that character is what we are when nobody is watching. How true. When we do things that we know aren't right, we try to hide them from our families and friends. But even if we successfully conceal our sins from the world, we can never conceal our sins from God.

If you sincerely wish to walk with your Creator, follow His commandments. When you do, your character will take care of itself . . . and you won't need to look over your shoulder to see who, besides God, is watching.

Maintaining your integrity in a world of sham
is no small accomplishment.

Wayne Oates

PRIORITIES FOR MY LIFE

One of your greatest possessions is integrity . . . don't lose it. Billy Graham was right when he said: "Integrity is the glue that holds our way of life together. We must constantly strive to keep our integrity intact. When wealth is lost, nothing is lost; when health is lost, something is lost; when character is lost, all is lost."

TIMELESS WISDOM FOR GODLY LIVING

The life of a good religious person ought to abound in every virtue so that he is, on the interior, what to others he appears to be.

Thomas à Kempis

In matters of style, swim with the current. In matters of principle, stand like a rock.

Thomas Jefferson

The man who cannot believe in himself cannot believe in anything else. The basis of all integrity and character is whatever faith we have in our own integrity.

Roy L. Smith

Integrity is not a given factor in everyone's life. It is a result of self-discipline, inner trust, and a decision to be relentlessly honest in all situations in our lives.

John Maxwell

> *People with integrity have firm footing,*
> *but those who follow crooked paths will slip and fall.*
> Proverbs 10:9 NLT

There's nothing like the power of integrity. It is a characteristic so radiant, so steady, so consistent, so beautiful, that it makes a permanent picture in our minds.

Franklin Graham

MORE WORDS FROM GOD'S WORD

The integrity of the upright will guide them.

Proverbs 11:3 NKJV

Love and truth form a good leader; sound leadership is founded on loving integrity.

Proverbs 20:28 MSG

May integrity and uprightness protect me, because my hope is in you.

Psalm 25:21 NIV

In everything set them an example by doing what is good. In your teaching show integrity, seriousness and soundness of speech that cannot be condemned, so that those who oppose you may be ashamed because they have nothing bad to say about us.

Titus 2:7 NIV

MY PRIORITIES FOR LIFE

I value the importance of being truthful with other people and with myself.

I will trust my conscience and follow it.

I will resist the temptation to follow the crowd, choosing instead to follow Jesus.

Check Your Priority		
High	Med.	Low
—	—	—
—	—	—
—	—	—

In a World Filled With Temptations

No temptation has seized you except what is common to man. And God is faithful; he will not let you be tempted beyond what you can bear. But when you are tempted, he will also provide a way out so that you can stand up under it.

1 Corinthians 10:13 NIV

Because our world is filled with temptations, we confront them at every turn. Some of these temptations are small—eating a second piece of chocolate cake, for example. Too much cake may cause us to defile, at least in a modest way, the bodily temple that God has entrusted to our care. But two pieces of cake will not bring us to our knees. Other temptations, however, are not so harmless.

The devil, it seems, is working overtime these days, and causing heartache in more places and in more ways than ever before. We, as Christians, must remain vigilant. Not only must we resist Satan when he confronts us, but we must also avoid those places where Satan can most easily tempt us. And, if we are to avoid the unending temptations of this world, we must arm ourselves with the Word of God.

In a letter to believers, Peter offered a stern warning: "Be sober, be vigilant; because your adversary the devil walks about like a roaring lion, seeking whom he may devour." (1 Peter 5:8 NKJV). What was true in New Testament times is equally true in our own. Satan tempts his prey and then devours them. And in these dangerous times, the tools that Satan uses to destroy his prey are more numerous than ever before.

As believing Christians, we must beware. And, if we seek righteousness in our own lives, we must earnestly wrap ourselves in the protection of God's Holy Word. After fasting forty days and nights in the desert, Jesus Himself was tempted by Satan. Christ used scripture to rebuke the devil (Matthew 4:1-11). We must do likewise. The Holy Bible provides us with a perfect blueprint for righteous living. If we consult that blueprint daily and follow it carefully, we build our lives according to God's plan. And when we do, we are secure.

It is easier to stay out of temptation than to get out of it.

Rick Warren

PRIORITIES FOR MY LIFE

You live in a "Temptation Nation." At every turn in the road, or so it seems, somebody is trying to tempt you with something. Your job is to steer clear of temptation . . . and to keep steering clear as long as you live.

TIMELESS WISDOM FOR GODLY LIVING

True peace of heart, then, is found in resisting passions, not in satisfying them.

Thomas à Kempis

Deception is the enemy's ongoing plan of attack.

Stormie Omartian

We have both help to endure temptation and pardon when we fall into it—we have every remedy for sin. We have Jesus.

Franklin Graham

The man of pleasure, by a vain attempt to be more happy than any man can be, is often more miserable than most.

Charles Caleb Colton

*Stay awake and pray,
so that you won't enter into temptation.
The spirit is willing, but the flesh is weak.*
Matthew 26:41 Holman CSB

We can't stop the Adversary from whispering in our ears, but we can refuse to listen, and we can definitely refuse to respond.

Liz Curtis Higgs

MORE WORDS FROM GOD'S WORD

The Lord knows how to deliver the godly out of temptations.

2 Peter 2:9 NKJV

Put on the whole armor of God, that you may be able to stand against the wiles of the devil.

Ephesians 6:11 NKJV

This High Priest of ours understands our weaknesses, for he faced all of the same temptations we do, yet he did not sin.

Hebrews 4:15 NLT

The Spirit's law of life in Christ Jesus has set you free from the law of sin and of death.

Romans 8:2 Holman CSB

MY PRIORITIES FOR LIFE

I trust that God can help me overcome any temptation.

When faced with temptation, I see the importance of turning my thoughts and my prayers to God.

I try to avoid situations where I might be tempted.

Check Your Priority		
High	Med.	Low
—	—	—
—	—	—
—	—	—

The Beliefs That Shape Your Values

Again, this is God's command: to believe in his personally named Son,
Jesus Christ. He told us to love each other, in line with the original
command. As we keep his commands, we live deeply and surely in him,
and he lives in us. And this is how we experience his deep
and abiding presence in us: by the Spirit he gave us.

1 John 3:23-24 MSG

In describing our beliefs, our actions are far better descriptors than our words. Yet far too many of us spend more energy talking about our beliefs than living by them—with predictably poor results.

As believers, we must beware: Our actions should always give credence to the changes that Christ can make in the lives of those who walk with Him.

Your beliefs shape your values, and your values shape your life. Is your life a clearly-crafted picture book of your creed? Are your actions always consistent with your beliefs? Are you willing to practice the philosophies that you preach? Hopefully so; otherwise, you'll be tormented by inconsistencies between your beliefs and your behaviors.

If you'd like to partake in the peace that only God can give, make certain that your actions are guided by His Word. And while you're at it, pay careful attention to the conscience that God, in His infinite wisdom, has placed in your heart. Don't treat your faith as if it were separate from your everyday life. Weave your beliefs into the very fabric of your day. When you do, God will honor your good works, and your good works will honor God.

If you seek to be a responsible believer, you must realize that it is never enough to hear the instructions of God; you must also live by them. And it is never enough to wait idly by while others do God's work here on earth; you, too, must act. Doing God's work is a responsibility that every Christian (including you) should bear. And when you do, your loving Heavenly Father will reward your efforts with a bountiful harvest.

As the body lives by breathing, so the soul lives by believing.

Thomas Brooks

PRIORITIES FOR MY LIFE

Talking about your beliefs is easy. But, making your actions match your words is much harder. Nevertheless, if you really want to be honest with yourself, then you must make your actions match your beliefs. Period.

TIMELESS WISDOM FOR GODLY LIVING

It is so hard to believe because it is so hard to obey.

Søren Kierkegaard

Forgive us our lack of faith, lest ulcers become our badge of disbelief.

Peter Marshall

Those who believe they believe in God but without passion in the heart, without anguish of mind, without uncertainty, without doubt, and even at times without despair, believe only in the idea of God, and not in God himself.

Madeleine L'Engle

Belief is not the result of an intellectual act; it is the result of an act of my will whereby I deliberately commit myself.

Oswald Chambers

Whoever believes that Jesus is the Christ is born of God, and everyone who loves Him who begot also loves him who is begotten of Him.

1 John 5:1 NKJV

If you believe those four words, "In the beginning God," you have no problem believing all the Bible.

Raymond Barber

MORE WORDS FROM GOD'S WORD

Jesus summed it all up when he cried out, "Whoever believes in me, believes not just in me but in the One who sent me. Whoever looks at me is looking, in fact, at the One who sent me. I am Light that has come into the world so that all who believe in me won't have to stay any longer in the dark."

John 12:44-46 MSG

Then He said to Thomas, "Put your finger here and observe My hands. Reach out your hand and put it into My side. Don't be an unbeliever, but a believer."

John 20:27 Holman CSB

Then Jesus told the centurion, "Go. As you have believed, let it be done for you." And his servant was cured that very moment.

Matthew 8:13 Holman CSB

MY PRIORITIES FOR LIFE

	Check Your Priority		
	High	Med.	Low
I understand that my beliefs will shape my values and my life.	—	—	—
I understand the importance of making my actions consistent with my beliefs.	—	—	—
When I struggle with my faith or with my behavior, I take those struggles to God.	—	—	—

Patience and Trust

Knowing God leads to self-control. Self-control leads to
patient endurance, and patient endurance leads to godliness.

2 Peter 1:6 NLT

The dictionary defines the word patience as "the ability to be calm, tolerant, and understanding." If that describes you, you can skip the rest of this page. But, if you're like most of us, you'd better keep reading.

For most of us, patience is a hard thing to master. Why? Because we have lots of things we want, and we know precisely when we want them: NOW (if not sooner). But our Father in heaven has other ideas; the Bible teaches that we must learn to wait patiently for the things that God has in store for us, even when waiting is difficult.

We live in an imperfect world inhabited by imperfect people. Sometimes, we inherit troubles from others, and sometimes we create troubles for ourselves. On other occasions, we see other people "moving ahead" in the world, and we want to move ahead with them. So we become impatient with ourselves, with our circumstances, and even with our Creator.

Psalm 37:7 commands us to "rest in the Lord, and wait patiently for Him" (NKJV). But, for most of us, waiting patiently for Him is hard. We are fallible human beings who seek solutions to our problems today, not tomorrow. Still, God instructs us to wait patiently for His plans to unfold, and that's exactly what we should do.

Sometimes, patience is the price we pay for being responsible adults, and that's as it should be. After all, think how patient our heavenly Father has been with us. So the next time you find yourself drumming your fingers as you wait for a quick resolution to the challenges of everyday living, take a deep breath and ask God for patience. Be still before your Heavenly Father and trust His timetable: it's the peaceful way to live.

Be patient. God is using today's difficulties
to strengthen you for tomorrow. He is equipping you.
The God who makes things grow will help you bear fruit.

Max Lucado

PRIORITIES FOR MY LIFE

The Best Things in Life Seldom Happen Overnight: They Usually Take Time: Henry Blackaby writes, "The grass that is here today and gone tomorrow does not require much time to mature. A big oak tree that lasts for generations requires much more time to grow and mature. God is concerned about your life through eternity. Allow Him to take all the time He needs to shape you for His purposes. Larger assignments will require longer periods of preparation." How true!

TIMELESS WISDOM FOR GODLY LIVING

Let me encourage you to continue to wait with faith. God may not perform a miracle, but He is trustworthy to touch you and make you whole where there used to be a hole.

Lisa Whelchel

There is no place for faith if we expect God to fulfill immediately what he promises.

John Calvin

In times of uncertainty, wait. Always, if you have any doubt, wait. Do not force yourself to any action. If you have a restraint in your spirit, wait until all is clear, and do not go against it.

Mrs. Charles E. Cowman

> *Now we exhort you, brethren,*
> *warn those who are unruly, comfort the fainthearted,*
> *uphold the weak, be patient with all.*
> 1 Thessalonians 5:14 NKJV

Let God use times of waiting to mold and shape your character. Let God use those times to purify your life and make you into a clean vessel for His service.

Henry Blackaby and Claude King

MORE WORDS FROM GOD'S WORD

Patience of spirit is better than haughtiness of spirit.

Ecclesiastes 7:8 NASB

God has chosen you and made you his holy people. He loves you. So always do these things: Show mercy to others, be kind, humble, gentle, and patient.

Colossians 3:12 NCV

And the servant of the Lord must not strive; but be gentle unto all men, apt to teach, patient; in meekness instructing those that oppose themselves . . . .

2 Timothy 2:24-25 KJV

Patience is better than strength.

Proverbs 16:32 ICB

MY PRIORITIES FOR LIFE

	Check Your Priority	
High	Med.	Low

I take seriously the Bible's instructions to be patient.

| — | — | — |

I believe that patience is not idly waiting, but that it is an activity that means watching and waiting for God to lead me.

| — | — | — |

Even when I don't understand the circumstances that confront me, I strive to wait patiently while serving the Lord.

| — | — | — |

Finding the Balance

But those who wait on the Lord Shall renew their strength;
They shall mount up with wings like eagles,
They shall run and not be weary, They shall walk and not faint.

Isaiah 40:31 NKJV

Face the facts: life is a delicate balancing act, a tightrope walk with over-commitment on one side and under-commitment on the other. And it's up to each of us to walk carefully on that rope, not falling prey to pride (which causes us to attempt too much) or to fear (which causes us to attempt too little).

God's Word promises us the possibility of abundance (John 10:10). And we are far more likely to experience that abundance when we lead balanced lives.

When you allow yourself to take on too many jobs, you simply can't do all of them well. That means that if you allow yourself to become overcommitted, whether at home, at work, at church, or anywhere in between, you're asking for trouble. So you must learn how to say no to the things you don't have the time or the energy to do.

Of course, sometimes, saying no can be tough. Why? Because well-meaning men (like you) genuinely want to help other people out. But if you allow your cart to become overworked, you may begin over-promising and under-serving—and you'll disappoint just about everybody, including yourself.

Are you and your loved ones doing too much—or too little? If so, it's time to have a little chat with God. And if you listen carefully to His instructions, you will strive to achieve a more balanced life, a life that's right for you and your loved ones. When you do, everybody wins.

When I feel like circumstances are spiraling downward in my life,
God taught me that whether I'm right side up or upside down,
I need to turn those circumstances over to Him.
He is the only one who can bring balance into my life.

Carole Lewis

PRIORITIES FOR MY LIFE

Need balance? Have a daily planning session with God. A regularly scheduled time of prayer, Bible reading, and meditation can help you prioritize your day and your life. And what if you're simply too busy to spend five or ten minutes with God? If so, it's time to reorder your priorities.

TIMELESS WISDOM FOR GODLY LIVING

We are all created differently. We share a common need to balance the different parts of our lives.

Dr. Walt Larimore

To do too much is as dangerous as to do nothing at all. Both modes prevent us from savoring our moments. One causes me to rush right past the best of life without recognizing or basking in it, and the other finds me sitting quietly as life rushes past me.

Patsy Clairmont

Does God care about all the responsibilities we have to juggle in our daily lives? Of course. But he cares more that our lives demonstrate balance, the ability to discern what is essential and give ourselves fully to it.

Penelope Stokes

It is better to be patient than powerful;
it is better to have self-control than to conquer a city.
Proverbs 16:32 NLT

Every one of us is supposed to be a powerhouse for God, living in balance and harmony within and without.

Joyce Meyer

MORE WORDS FROM GOD'S WORD

Then the apostles gathered to Jesus and told Him all things, both what they had done and what they had taught. And He said to them, "Come aside by yourselves to a deserted place and rest a while." For there were many coming and going, and they did not even have time to eat.

Mark 6:30-31 NKJV

Come to Me, all you who labor and are heavy laden, and I will give you rest. Take My yoke upon you and learn from Me, for I am gentle and lowly in heart, and you will find rest for your souls. For My yoke is easy and My burden is light.

Matthew 11:28-30 NKJV

But take heed to yourselves, lest your hearts be weighed down with carousing, drunkenness, and cares of this life.

Luke 21:34 NKJV

MY PRIORITIES FOR LIFE

Accepting God's will (even when I don't understand it) has a value that is . . .

	Check Your Priority	
High	Med.	Low
—	—	—

I am willing to work to resolve my problems, yet I am also willing to wait patiently for God to respond to my prayers.

—	—	—

Enthusiasm for Life

Whatever you do, do it enthusiastically,
as something done for the Lord and not for men.

Colossians 3:23 Holman CSB

Can you honestly say that you are an enthusiastic believer? Are you passionate about your faith and excited about your path? Hopefully so. But if your zest for life has waned, it is now time to redirect your efforts and recharge your spiritual batteries. And that means refocusing your values by putting God first.

Nothing is more important than your wholehearted commitment to your Creator and to His only begotten Son. Your faith must never be an afterthought; it must be your ultimate priority, your ultimate possession, and your ultimate passion. When you become passionate about your faith, you'll become passionate about your life, too.

Norman Vincent Peale advised, "Get absolutely enthralled with something. Throw yourself into it with abandon. Get out of yourself. Be somebody. Do something." His words still ring true. But sometimes, when the stresses of everyday life seem overwhelming, you may not feel very enthusiastic about your life or yourself. If so, it's time to reorder your thoughts, your priorities, your values, and your prayers. When you do, you'll not only be helping yourself, but you'll also be helping your family and friends.

Genuine, heartfelt, enthusiastic Christianity is contagious. If you enjoy a life-altering relationship with God, that relationship will have an impact on others—perhaps a profound impact.

Are you genuinely excited about your faith? And do you make your enthusiasm known to those around you? Or are you satisfied to be a "silent ambassador" for Christ? God's preference is clear: He intends that you stand before others and proclaim your faith.

Remember: You are the recipient of Christ's sacrificial love. Accept it enthusiastically and share it passionately. Jesus deserves your enthusiasm; the world deserves it; and you deserve the experience of sharing it.

There seems to be a chilling fear of holy enthusiasm
among the people of God. We try to tell how happy we are—
but we remain so well-controlled that there are
very few waves of glory experienced in our midst.

A. W. Tozer

PRIORITIES FOR MY LIFE

Don't wait for enthusiasm to find you . . . go looking for it. Look at your life and your relationships as exciting adventures. Don't wait for life to spice itself; spice things up yourself.

TIMELESS WISDOM FOR GODLY LIVING

Enthusiasm, like the flu, is contagious—we get it from one another.

Barbara Johnson

We act as though comfort and luxury were the chief requirements of life, when all we need to make us really happy is something to be enthusiastic about.

Charles Kingsley

Don't take hold of a thing unless you want that thing to take hold of you.

E. Stanley Jones

Wherever you are, be all there. Live to the hilt every situation you believe to be the will of God.

Jim Elliot

> *Never be lazy in your work,*
> *but serve the Lord enthusiastically.*
> Romans 12:11 NLT

When we wholeheartedly commit ourselves to God, there is nothing mediocre or run-of-the-mill about us. To live for Christ is to be passionate about our Lord and about our lives.

Jim Gallery

MORE WORDS FROM GOD'S WORD

Whatever work you do, do your best, because you are going to the grave, where there is no working . . . .

Ecclesiastes 9:10 NCV

I have seen that there is nothing better than for a person to enjoy his activities, because that is his reward. For who can enable him to see what will happen after he dies?

Ecclesiastes 3:22 Holman CSB

Do your work with enthusiasm. Work as if you were serving the Lord, not as if you were serving only men and women.

Ephesians 6:7 NCV

Let the hearts of those who seek the Lord rejoice. Look to the Lord and his strength; seek his face always.

1 Chronicles 16:10-11 NIV

MY PRIORITIES FOR LIFE

	Check Your Priority	
High	Med.	Low

My faith gives me reason to be enthusiastic about life.

— — —

For me, it is important to generate enthusiastic thoughts.

— — —

When I praise God and thank Him for His blessings, I feel enthusiastic about life.

— — —

The Words We Speak

So then, rid yourselves of all evil, all lying, hypocrisy,
jealousy, and evil speech. As newborn babies want milk,
you should want the pure and simple teaching.
By it you can grow up and be saved.

1 Peter 2:1–2 NCV

How much value do you place on the words you speak? Hopefully, you understand that your words have great power . . . because they most certainly do. If your words are encouraging, you can lift others up; if your words are hurtful, you can hold others back.

The Bible makes it clear that "Reckless words pierce like a sword, but the tongue of the wise brings healing" (Proverbs 12:18 NIV). So, if you hope to solve problems instead of starting them, you must measure your words carefully. But sometimes, you'll be tempted to speak first and think second (with decidedly mixed results).

When you're frustrated or tired, you may say things that would be better left unspoken. Whenever you lash out in anger, you forgo the wonderful opportunity to consider your thoughts before you give voice to them. When you speak impulsively, you may, quite unintentionally, injure others.

A far better strategy, of course, is to do the more difficult thing: to think first and to speak next. When you do so, you give

yourself ample time to compose your thoughts and to consult
your Creator (but not necessarily in that order!).

The Bible warns that you will be judged by the words you
speak (Matthew 12:36-37). And, Ephesians 4:29 instructs you to
make "each word a gift" (MSG). These passages make it clear that
God cares very much about the things you say and the way you
say them. And if God cares that much, so should you.

Do you seek to be a source of encouragement to others? Are
you a beacon of hope to your friends and family? And, do you
seek to be a worthy ambassador for Christ? If so, you must speak
words that are worthy of your Savior. So avoid angry outbursts.
Refrain from impulsive outpourings. Terminate tantrums.
Instead, speak words of encouragement and hope to a world that
desperately needs both.

Fill the heart with the love of Christ so that
only truth and purity can come out of the mouth.

Warren Wiersbe

PRIORITIES FOR MY LIFE

Words, words, words . . . are important, important, important!
So make sure that you think first and speak next. Otherwise, you
may give the greatest speech you wish you'd never made!

TIMELESS WISDOM FOR GODLY LIVING

In all your deeds and words, you should look on Jesus as your model, whether you are keeping silence or speaking, whether you are alone or with others.

St. Bonaventure

When you talk, choose the very same words that you would use if Jesus were looking over your shoulder. Because He is.

Marie T. Freeman

We will always experience regret when we live for the moment and do not weigh our words and deeds before we give them life.

Lisa Bevere

A little kindly advice is better than a great deal of scolding.

Fanny Crosby

> *Be gracious in your speech. The goal is to bring out the best in others in a conversation, not put them down, not cut them out.*
>
> Colossians 4:6 MSG

Like dynamite, God's power is only latent power until it is released. You can release God's dynamite power into people's lives and the world through faith, your words, and prayer.

Bill Bright

MORE WORDS FROM GOD'S WORD

To everything there is a season . . . a time to keep silence, and a time to speak.

Ecclesiastes 3:1,7 KJV

Watch the way you talk. Let nothing foul or dirty come out of your mouth. Say only what helps, each word a gift.

Ephesians 4:29 MSG

If anyone considers himself religious and yet does not keep a tight rein on his tongue, he deceives himself and his religion is worthless.

James 1:26 NIV

For the one who wants to love life and to see good days must keep his tongue from evil and his lips from speaking deceit.

1 Peter 3:10 Holman CSB

MY PRIORITIES FOR LIFE

Every day, I try to find at least one person to encourage.

I believe that my words are important, so I try to think before I speak, not after.

I find that when I encourage others, I too, am encouraged.

Check Your Priority		
High	Med.	Low
—	—	—
—	—	—
—	—	—

Making Choices That Please God

Choose for yourselves today the one you will worship . . . .
As for me and my family, we will worship the Lord.

Joshua 24:15 Holman CSB

From the instant we wake in the morning until the moment we nod off to sleep at night, we make countless choices: choices about the things we do, choices about the words we speak, even subtle choices about the way we direct our thoughts. Simply put, the quality of those choices determines the quality of our lives.

As believers who have been saved by a loving and merciful God, we have every reason to make wise choices. Yet sometimes, amid the inevitable hustle and bustle of life-here-on-earth, we allow ourselves to behave in ways that we know are displeasing to our Creator. When we do, we forfeit the joy and the peace that we might otherwise experience through Him.

Sometimes, because you're an imperfect human being, you may become so wrapped up in meeting society's expectations that you fail to focus on God's expectations. To do so is a mistake of major proportions—don't make it.

Whom will you try to please today: God or man? Your primary obligation is not to please imperfect men and women.

Your obligation is to strive diligently to meet the expectations of an all-knowing and perfect God. Trust Him always. Love Him always. Praise Him always. And make choices that please Him. Always.

Life is pretty much like a cafeteria line—it offers us many choices, both good and bad. The Christian must have a spiritual radar that detects the difference not only between bad and good but also among good, better, and best.

Dennis Swanberg

PRIORITIES FOR MY LIFE

Whose plans? God's plans! If you have been struggling against God's will for your life, you have invited unwelcome consequences into your own life and into the lives of your loved ones. A far better strategy is to consult God earnestly and often. God's plans are the best plans for you.

TIMELESS WISDOM FOR GODLY LIVING

Many jokes are made about the devil, but the devil is no joke. He is called a deceiver. In order to accomplish his purpose, the devil blinds people to their need for Christ. Two forces are at work in our world—the forces of Christ and the forces of the devil—and you are asked to choose.

Billy Graham

You should forget about trying to be popular with everybody and start trying to be popular with God Almighty.

Sam Jones

We are either the masters or the victims of our attitudes. It is a matter of personal choice. Who we are today is the result of choices we made yesterday. Tomorrow, we will become what we choose today. To change means to choose to change.

John Maxwell

Teach me Your way, O Lord; I will walk in Your truth.
Psalm 86:11 NKJV

All our offerings, whether music or martyrdom, are like the intrinsically worthless present of a child, which a father values indeed, but values only for the intention.

C. S. Lewis

MORE WORDS FROM GOD'S WORD

*It is God who is at work in you, both to will and to work for His good
pleasure.*

Philippians 2:13 NASB

. . . not my will, but thine, be done.

Luke 22:42 KJV

*Obviously, I'm not trying to be a people pleaser! No, I am trying to please
God. If I were still trying to please people, I would not be Christ's servant.*

Galatians 1:10 NLT

*Our only goal is to please God whether we live here or there, because we
must all stand before Christ to be judged.*

2 Corinthians 5:9-10 NCV

MY PRIORITIES FOR LIFE

I place importance on making choices that are
pleasing to God.

I trust that I can please God by being obedient
to His Word.

I believe that by making wise choices, I demonstrate
my love for God.

Check Your Priority		
High	Med.	Low
—	—	—
—	—	—
—	—	—

Making Praise a Priority

Is anyone happy? Let him sing songs of praise.

James 5:13 NIV

When is the best time to praise God? In church? Before dinner is served? When we tuck little children into bed? None of the above. The best time to praise God is all day, every day, to the greatest extent we can, with thanksgiving in our hearts, and with a song on our lips.

Too many of us, even well-intentioned believers, tend to "compartmentalize" our waking hours into a few familiar categories: work, rest, play, family time, and worship. To do so is a mistake. Worship and praise should be woven into the fabric of everything we do; it should never be relegated to a weekly three-hour visit to church on Sunday morning.

The words by Fanny Crosby are familiar: "This is my story, this is my song, praising my Savior, all the day long." As believers who have been saved by the sacrifice of a risen Christ, we must do exactly as the song instructs: We must praise our Savior time and time again throughout the day. Worship and praise should be a part of everything we do. Otherwise, we quickly lose perspective as we fall prey to the demands of everyday life.

Theologian Wayne Oates once admitted, "Many of my prayers are made with my eyes open. You see, it seems I'm always praying about something, and it's not always convenient—or safe—to close my eyes." Dr. Oates understood that God always hears our prayers and that the relative position of our eyelids is of no concern to Him.

Do you sincerely desire to be a worthy servant of the One who has given you eternal love and eternal life? Then praise Him for who He is and for what He has done for you. And don't just praise Him on Sunday morning. Praise Him all day long, every day, for as long as you live . . . and then for all eternity.

I am to praise God for all things, regardless of where they seem to originate. Doing this is the key to receiving the blessings of God. Praise will wash away my resentments.

Catherine Marshall

PRIORITIES FOR MY LIFE

Thoughtful believers (like you) make it a habit to carve out quiet moments throughout the day to praise God.

TIMELESS WISDOM FOR GODLY LIVING

The time for universal praise is sure to come some day. Let us begin to do our part now.

Hannah Whitall Smith

Praise and thank God for who He is and for what He has done for you.

Billy Graham

Praise Him! Praise Him! Tell of His excellent greatness. Praise Him! Praise Him! Ever in joyful song!

Fanny Crosby

Stand up and bless the Lord, ye people of his choice; stand up and bless the Lord your God with heart and soul and voice.

James Montgomery

*Through Him then, let us continually offer up
a sacrifice of praise to God, that is,
the fruit of lips that give thanks to His name.*
Hebrews 13:15 NASB

Maintaining a focus on God will take our praise to heights that nothing else can.

Jeff Walling

MORE WORDS FROM GOD'S WORD

The LORD is my strength and song, and He has become my salvation; He is my God, and I will praise Him.

Exodus 15:2 NIV

And suddenly there was with the angel a multitude of the heavenly host praising God and saying: "Glory to God in the highest, And on earth peace, goodwill toward men!"

Luke 2:13-14 NKJV

At the name of Jesus every knee should bow, of those in heaven, and of those on earth, and of those under the earth, and that every tongue should confess that Jesus Christ is Lord, to the glory of God the Father.

Philippians 2:10-11 NKJV

MY PRIORITIES FOR LIFE

I make it a habit to praise God many times each day, beginning with my morning devotional.

Whether I am experiencing good times or difficult times, I understand the need to praise God.

When I praise God, I feel that I am following in the footsteps of His Son.

Check Your Priority		
High	Med.	Low
—	—	—
—	—	—
—	—	—

Above and Beyond Our Worries

So do not worry, saying, "What shall we eat?" or "What shall we drink?"
or "What shall we wear?" For the pagans run after all these things,
and your heavenly Father knows that you need them. But seek first
his kingdom and his righteousness, and all these things will be given to
you as well. Therefore do not worry about tomorrow, for tomorrow
will worry about itself. Each day has enough trouble of its own.

Matthew 6:31-34 NIV

If you are a man with lots of obligations and plenty of responsibilities, it is simply a fact of life: You worry. From time to time, you worry about health, about finances, about safety, about family, and about countless other concerns, some great and some small.

Where is the best place to take your worries? Take them to God. Take your troubles to Him; take your fears to Him; take your doubts to Him; take your weaknesses to Him; take your sorrows to Him . . . and leave them all there. Seek protection from the One who offers you eternal salvation; build your spiritual house upon the Rock that cannot be moved.

Perhaps you are uncertain about your future or your finances—or perhaps you are simply a "worrier" by nature. If so, it's time to focus less on your troubles and more on God's

promises. And that's as it should be because God is trustworthy
. . . and you are protected.

Worry is a complete waste of energy. It solves nothing.
And it won't solve that anxiety on your mind either.

Charles Swindoll

Because God is my sovereign Lord, I was not worried.
He manages perfectly, day and night, year in and year out,
the movements of the stars, the wheeling of the planets,
the staggering coordination of events that goes on at
the molecular level in order to hold things together.
There is no doubt that he can manage the timing
of my days and weeks.

Elisabeth Elliot

PRIORITIES FOR MY LIFE

Carefully divide your areas of concern into two categories:
the things you can control and the things you cannot control.
Resolve never to waste time or energy worrying about the latter.

TIMELESS WISDOM FOR GODLY LIVING

Worry does not empty tomorrow of its sorrow; it empties today of its strength.

Corrie ten Boom

Today is the tomorrow we worried about yesterday.

Dennis Swanberg

It has been well said that no man ever sank under the burden of the day. It is when tomorrow's burden is added to the burden of today that the weight is more than a man can bear. Never load yourselves so, my friends. If you find yourselves so loaded, at least remember this: it is your own doing, not God's. He begs you to leave the future to Him and mind the present.

George MacDonald

Come to Me, all you who labor and are heavy laden, and I will give you rest. Take My yoke upon you and learn from Me, for I am gentle and lowly in heart, and you will find rest for your souls. For My yoke is easy and My burden is light.
Matthew 11:28-30 NKJV

The beginning of anxiety is the end of faith, and the beginning of true faith is the end of anxiety.

George Mueller

MORE WORDS FROM GOD'S WORD

I was very worried, but you comforted me . . . .

Psalm 94:19 NCV

An anxious heart weighs a man down....

Proverbs 12:25 NIV

Jesus said, "Don't let your hearts be troubled. Trust in God, and trust in me."

John 14:1 NCV

Yea, though I walk through the valley of the shadow of death, I will fear no evil: for thou art with me; thy rod and thy staff they comfort me.

Psalm 23:4 KJV

MY PRIORITIES FOR LIFE

I believe that it is important to try to live in "day-tight" compartments by not fretting too much about yesterday or tomorrow.

I use prayer as an antidote to worry.

When I am worried, I try to think of things that I can do to help solve the things that trouble me.

Check Your Priority		
High	Med.	Low
—	—	—
—	—	—
—	—	—

The Wisdom to be Humble

Finally, all of you should be of one mind,
full of sympathy toward each other,
loving one another with tender hearts and humble minds.

1 Peter 3:8 NLT

Are you a humble believer who always gives credit where credit is due? If so, you are both wise and blessed.

Dietrich Bonhoeffer observed, "It is very easy to overestimate the importance of our own achievements in comparison with what we owe others." How true. Even those of us who consider ourselves "self-made" men and women are deeply indebted to more people than we can count. Our first and greatest indebtedness, of course, is to God and His only begotten Son. But we are also indebted to ancestors, parents, teachers, friends, spouses, family members, coworkers, fellow believers . . . and the list goes on.

With so many people who rightfully deserve to share the credit for our successes, how can we gloat? The answer, of course, is that we should not. But we inhabit a world in which far too many of our role models are remarkably haughty and surprisingly self-centered (hopefully, these are not your role models).

The Bible contains stern warnings against the sin of pride. One such warning is found in Proverbs 16:8: "Pride goes before destruction, and a haughty spirit before a fall" (NKJV). God's Word makes it clear: pride and destruction are traveling companions (but hopefully, they're not your traveling companions).

Jonathan Edwards observed, "Nothing sets a person so much out of the devil's reach as humility." So, if you're celebrating a worthwhile accomplishment, don't invite the devil to celebrate with you. Instead of puffing out your chest and saying, "Look at me!" give credit where credit is due, starting with God. And rest assured: There is no such thing as a self-made man. All of us are made by God . . . and He deserves the glory, not us.

Do you wish to be great? Then begin by being humble.
Do you desire to construct a vast and lofty fabric?
Think first about the foundations of humility. The higher
your structure is to be, the deeper must be its foundation.

St. Augustine

PRIORITIES FOR MY LIFE

If you're going to make fun of somebody . . . let it be yourself. You can't really laugh with other people until they know you're willing to laugh at yourself.

TIMELESS WISDOM FOR GODLY LIVING

Humility is not thinking less of yourself; it is thinking of yourself less.

Rick Warren

The great characteristic of the saint is humility.

Oswald Chambers

God exalts humility. When God works in our lives, helping us to become humble, he gives us a permanent joy. Humility gives us a joy that cannot be taken away.

Max Lucado

Nothing sets a person so much out of the devil's reach as humility.

Jonathan Edwards

God is against the proud,
but he gives grace to the humble.
1 Peter 5:5 NCV

Let Christ be formed in me, and let me learn of him all lowliness of heart, all gentleness of bearing, all modesty of speech, all helpfulness of action, and promptness in the doing of my Father's will.

John Baillie

MORE WORDS FROM GOD'S WORD

Therefore humble yourselves under the mighty hand of God, that He may exalt you at the proper time, casting all your anxiety on Him, because He cares for you.

1 Peter 5:6-7 NASB

God has chosen you and made you his holy people. He loves you. So always do these things: Show mercy to others, be kind, humble, gentle, and patient.

Colossians 3:12 NCV

You will save the humble people; But Your eyes are on the haughty, that You may bring them down.

2 Samuel 22:28 NKJV

MY PRIORITIES FOR LIFE

I understand the importance of humbly acknowledging God's blessings.

I will gratefully acknowledge those people who have helped me accomplish my goals.

I will refrain from boastful displays, and I will not attempt to "keep up with the Joneses."

I will strive to give credit where credit is due . . . starting with God.

Check Your Priority		
High	Med.	Low
—	—	—
—	—	—
—	—	—
—	—	—

The Source of Strength

Be strong! We must prove ourselves strong for our people
and for the cities of our God. May the Lord's will be done.

1 Chronicles 19:13 Holman CSB

Even the most inspired Christians can, from time to time, find themselves running on empty. The demands of daily life can drain us of our strength and rob us of the joy that is rightfully ours in Christ. When we find ourselves tired, discouraged, or worse, there is a source from which we can draw the power needed to recharge our spiritual batteries. That source is God.

God intends that His children lead joyous lives filled with abundance and peace. But sometimes, abundance and peace seem very far away. It is then that we must turn to God for renewal, and when we do, He will restore us if we allow Him to do so.

Today, like every other day, is literally brimming with possibilities. Whether we realize it or not, God is always working in us and through us; our job is to let Him do His work without undo interference. Yet we are imperfect beings who, because of our limited vision, often resist God's will. And oftentimes, because of our stubborn insistence on squeezing too many activities into a 24-hour day, we allow ourselves to become exhausted, or frustrated, or both.

Are you tired or troubled? Turn your heart toward God in prayer. Are you weak or worried? Take the time—or, more accurately, make the time—to delve deeply into God's Holy Word. Are you spiritually depleted? Call upon fellow believers to support you, and call upon Christ to renew your spirit and your life. Are you simply overwhelmed by the demands of the day? Pray for the wisdom to simplify your life. Are you exhausted? Pray for the wisdom to rest a little more and worry a little less.

When you do these things, you'll discover that the Creator of the universe stands always ready and always able to create a new sense of wonderment and joy in you.

When I feel afraid, and think I've lost my way,
still You're right there beside me.
Nothing will I fear as long as You are near.

Amy Grant

PRIORITIES FOR MY LIFE

Need Strength? Let God's Spirit Reign Over Your Heart. Billy Graham writes, "One with God is a majority." And remember majority rules.

TIMELESS WISDOM FOR GODLY LIVING

God covers the distance between us with his own strength.

Angela Thomas

God is great and God is powerful, but we must invite him to be powerful in our lives. His strength is always there, but it's up to us to provide a channel through which that power can flow.

Bill Hybels

Prayer plumes the wings of God's young eaglets so that they may learn to mount above the clouds. Prayer brings inner strength to God's warriors and sends them forth to spiritual battle with their muscles firm and their armor in place.

C. H. Spurgeon

And He said to me, "My grace is sufficient for you, for My strength is made perfect in weakness."
2 Corinthians 12:9 NKJV

There are two things we are called to do: we are to depend on His strength and be obedient to His Word. If we can't handle being dependent and obedient, we will never become the kind of people who have a heart for God.

Stuart Briscoe

MORE WORDS FROM GOD'S WORD

Finally, be strengthened by the Lord and by His vast strength.

Ephesians 6:10 Holman CSB

The LORD is my strength and my song....

Exodus 15:2 NIV

Those who hope in the LORD will renew their strength. They will soar on wings like eagles; they will run and not grow weary, they will walk and not be faint.

Isaiah 40:31 NIV

Whatever your hand finds to do, do it with all your might....

Ecclesiastes 9:10 NIV

I can do all things through Him who strengthens me.

Philippians 4:13 NASB

MY PRIORITIES FOR LIFE

I believe that I gain strength when I allow Christ to dwell in the center of my heart.

I understand the importance of regular exercise and sensible rest.

I gain strength through prayer.

Check Your Priority		
High	Med.	Low
—	—	—
—	—	—
—	—	—

Walking in Truth

I have no greater joy than this:
to hear that my children are walking in the truth.

3 John 1:4 Holman CSB

Would you like a rock-solid, time-tested formula for success? Here it is: Seek God's truth, and live by it. Of course this strategy may sound simple, and it may sound somewhat old-fashioned, especially if you're a fast-track, dues-paying citizen of the 21st Century. But God's truth never goes out of style. And God's wisdom is as valid today as it was when He laid the foundations of the universe.

The familiar words of John 8:32 remind us that "you shall know the truth, and the truth shall make you free" (NKJV). And St. Augustine had this advice: "Let everything perish! Dismiss these empty vanities! And let us take up the search for the truth."

God is vitally concerned with truth. His Word teaches the truth; His Spirit reveals the truth; His Son leads us to the truth. When we open our hearts to God, and when we allow His Son to rule over our thoughts and our lives, God reveals Himself, and we come to understand the truth about ourselves and the truth about God's gift of grace.

Are you seeking God's truth and making decisions in light of that truth? Hopefully so. When you do, you'll discover that the truth will indeed set you free, now and forever.

Having a doctrine pass before the mind is not what
the Bible means by knowing the truth. It's only when it
reaches down deep into the heart that the truth begins
to set us free, just as a key must penetrate a lock to turn it,
or as rainfall must saturate the earth down to the roots
in order for your garden to grow.

John Eldredge

Truth will triumph. The Father of truth will win,
and the followers of truth will be saved.

Max Lucado

PRIORITIES FOR MY LIFE

Knowing God's truth is dramatically different from living it.
Make sure that you do both.

TIMELESS WISDOM FOR GODLY LIVING

God offers to everyone the choice between truth and repose. Take which you please, but you can never have both.

Ralph Waldo Emerson

Learning God's truth and getting it into our heads is one thing, but living God's truth and getting it into our characters is quite something else.

Warren Wiersbe

Peace, if possible, but truth at any rate.

Martin Luther

You have already heard about this hope in the message of truth, the gospel that has come to you. It is bearing fruit and growing all over the world, just as it has among you since the day you heard it and recognized God's grace in the truth.
Colossians 1:5-6 Holman CSB

Because a thing is eloquently expressed it should not be taken to be as necessarily true; nor because it is uttered with stammering lips should it be supposed false.

St. Augustine

MORE WORDS FROM GOD'S WORD

A person who does not have the Spirit does not accept the truths that come from the Spirit of God. That person thinks they are foolish and cannot understand them, because they can only be judged to be true by the Spirit. The spiritual person is able to judge all things, but no one can judge him.

1 Corinthians 2:14–15 NCV

Therefore laying aside falsehood, speak truth, each one of you, with his neighbor, for we are members of one another.

Ephesians 4:25 NASB

Be diligent to present yourself approved to God, a worker who doesn't need to be ashamed, correctly teaching the word of truth.

2 Timothy 2:15 Holman CSB

MY PRIORITIES FOR LIFE

I will do my best to be truthful with others and with myself.

I will seek God's truth.

I will strive to live in accordance with my beliefs.

Check Your Priority		
High	Med.	Low
—	—	—
—	—	—
—	—	—

Our Problems = God's Opportunities

Let not your heart be troubled:
ye believe in God, believe also in me.

John 14:1 KJV

Life is an adventure in problem-solving. The question is not whether we will encounter problems; the real question is how we will choose to address them. When it comes to solving the problems of everyday living, we often know precisely what needs to be done, but we may be slow in doing it—especially if what needs to be done is difficult. So we put off till tomorrow what should be done today.

As a man living here in the 21st-century, you have your own set of challenges. As you face those challenges, you may be comforted by this fact: Trouble, of every kind, is temporary. Yet, God's grace is eternal. And worries, of every kind, are temporary. But God's love is everlasting. The troubles that concern you will pass. God remains. And for every problem, God has a solution.

The words of Psalm 34 remind us that the Lord solves problems for "people who do what is right." And usually, doing "what is right" means doing the uncomfortable work of confronting our problems sooner rather than later. So with no further ado, let the problem-solving begin . . . right now.

God is bigger than your problems.
Whatever worries press upon you today,
put them in God's hands and leave them there.

Billy Graham

I have told you these things, so that in me you may have peace.
In this world you will have trouble.
But take heart! I have overcome the world.

John 16:33 NIV

PRIORITIES FOR MY LIFE

When it comes to solving problems, it's better to invest more
time working on them and less time fretting over them.

TIMELESS WISDOM FOR GODLY LIVING

Each problem is a God-appointed instructor.

Charles Swindoll

Life will be made or broken at the place where we meet and deal with obstacles.

E. Stanley Jones

The apostle Paul said we are to "bear one another's burdens," not "solve one another's problems."

Ed Young

Faith does not eliminate problems. Faith keeps you in a trusting relationship with God in the midst of your problems.

Henry Blackaby

People who do what is right may have many problems, but the Lord will solve them all.
Psalm 34:19 NCV

The happiest people in the world are not those who have no problems, but the people who have learned to live with those things that are less than perfect.

James Dobson

MORE WORDS FROM GOD'S WORD

Be joyful because you have hope. Be patient when trouble comes, and pray at all times.

Romans 12:12 NCV

When troubles come and all these awful things happen to you, in future days you will come back to God, your God, and listen obediently to what he says. God, your God, is above all a compassionate God. In the end he will not abandon you, he won't bring you to ruin, he won't forget the covenant with your ancestors which he swore to them.

Deuteronomy 4:30-31 MSG

When you go through deep waters and great trouble, I will be with you. When you go through the rivers of difficulty, you will not drown! When you walk through the fire of oppression, you will not be burned up; the flames will not consume you. For I am the Lord, your God . . . .

Isaiah 43:2-3 NLT

MY PRIORITIES FOR LIFE

When I encounter problems, I will also look for solutions.

When I encounter problems, I will tackle them sooner rather than later.

When I encounter problems, I will look at them as opportunities, not obstacles.

Check Your Priority		
High	Med.	Low
—	—	—
—	—	—
—	—	—

Your Plans . . . And God's

And we know that in all things God works for the good of those who love him, who have been called according to his purpose.

Romans 8:28 NIV

Are you willing to plan for the future—and are you willing to work diligently to accomplish the plans that you've made? If you desire to reap a bountiful harvest from life, you should plan for the future (by crafting a "to-do list for life") while entrusting the final outcome to God. Then, you should do your part to make the future better (by working dutifully), while acknowledging the sovereignty of God's hands over all affairs, including your own.

As you make plans and establish priorities, remember this: you're not the only one working on your behalf: God, too, is at work. And with Him as your partner, your ultimate success is guaranteed.

God has big plans for your life, wonderful, surprising plans . . . but He won't force those plans upon you. To the contrary, He has given you free will, the ability to make decisions on your own. Now, it's up to you to make those decisions wisely.

If you seek to live in accordance with God's plan for your life, you will study His Word, you will be attentive to His instructions, and you will be watchful for His signs. You will associate with fellow believers who, by their words and actions, will encourage your spiritual growth. You will assiduously avoid those two terrible temptations: the temptation to sin and the temptation to squander time. And finally, you will listen carefully, even reverently, to the conscience that God has placed in your heart.

God intends to use you in wonderful, unexpected ways if you let Him. Your job, of course, is to let Him.

The only way you can experience abundant life
is to surrender your plans to Him.

Charles Stanley

PRIORITIES FOR MY LIFE

Big, bigger, and very big plans: God has very big plans in store for your life, so trust Him and wait patiently for those plans to unfold. And remember: God's timing is best.

TIMELESS WISDOM FOR GODLY LIVING

Plan your work. Without a system, you'll feel swamped.

Norman Vincent Peale

Plan ahead—it wasn't raining when Noah built the ark.

Anonymous

Let our advance worrying become advance thinking and planning.

Winston Churchill

He who every morning plans the transactions of the day and follows out that plan carries a thread that will guide him through the labyrinth of the most busy life.

Victor Hugo

Teach me Your way, O Lord; I will walk in Your truth.
Psalm 86:11 NKJV

The future belongs to those who prepare for it.

Ralph Waldo Emerson

MORE WORDS FROM GOD'S WORD

Trust the Lord your God with all your heart and lean not on your own understanding; in all your ways acknowledge him, and he will make your paths straight.

Proverbs 3:5-6 NIV

There is one thing I always do. Forgetting the past and straining toward what is ahead, I keep trying to reach the goal and get the prize for which God called me . . . .

Philippians 3:13–14 NCV

I say this because I know what I am planning for you," says the Lord. "I have good plans for you, not plans to hurt you. I will give you hope and a good future."

Jeremiah 29:11 NCV

MY PRIORITIES FOR LIFE

Since I trust that God's plans have eternal ramifications, I will seek His will for my life.

Since I believe that God has a plan for my day, I set aside quiet time each morning in order to seek His will for my life.

My plans are imperfect; God's plans are perfect; so I choose to trust God.

Check Your Priority		
High	Med.	Low
—	—	—
—	—	—
—	—	—

A Passion for Life

He did it with all his heart. So he prospered.

2 Chronicles 31:21 NKJV

Have you discovered a life's work that excites you? Are you passionate about your career? Have you discovered something that makes you want to hop out of bed in the morning and get to work? And does that "something" make the world—and your world—a better place? If so, thank God every day for that blessing.

If you have not yet discovered work that blesses you and your world, don't allow yourself to become discouraged. Instead, keep searching and keep trusting that with God's help, you can—and will—find a meaningful way to serve your neighbors and your Creator.

The old adage is both familiar and true: We must pray as if everything depended upon God, but work as if everything depended upon us. Yet sometimes, when we find ourselves laboring in jobs that we don't enjoy, we may become lackadaisical about our responsibilities. God has other intentions. God expects us to work diligently and enthusiastically for the things we need (2 Thessalonians 3:10, Colossians 3:23).

Are you willing to work diligently for yourself, for your family, and for your God? And are you willing to engage in work that is pleasing to your Creator? If so, you can expect your Heavenly Father to bring forth a rich harvest.

And, if you have concerns about any aspect of your professional life, take those concerns to God in prayer. He will guide your steps, He will steady your hand, He will calm your fears, and He will reward your efforts.

Some of us simmer all our lives and never come to a boil.

Vance Havner

Let us live with urgency. Let us exploit the opportunity of life.
Let us not drift. Let us live intentionally.
We must not trifle our lives away.

Raymond Ortlund

PRIORITIES FOR MY LIFE

Involve yourself in activities that you can support wholeheartedly and enthusiastically. It's easier to celebrate life when you're passionately involved in life.

TIMELESS WISDOM FOR GODLY LIVING

But what hope have we if, while singing "Onward Christian Soldiers," we go through perfunctory services, parroting prayers, yawning over watches, acting as if we were excursionists on a pleasure expedition?

R. G. Lee

Get absolutely enthralled with something. Throw yourself into it with abandon. Get out of yourself. Be somebody. Do something.

Norman Vincent Peale

You don't have to advertise a fire. Get on fire for God and the world will come to watch you burn.

John Wesley

In all the work you are doing, work the best you can. Work as if you were doing it for the Lord, not for people.
Colossians 3:23 NCV

Today God's eyes are still running all across America . . . the world . . . looking for someone, anyone, who will totally and passionately seek him, who is determined that every thought and action will be pleasing in his sight. For such a person or group, God will prove himself mighty. His power will explode on their behalf.

Jim Cymbala

MORE WORDS FROM GOD'S WORD

I have seen that there is nothing better than for a person to enjoy his activities, because that is his reward. For who can enable him to see what will happen after he dies?

Ecclesiastes 3:22 Holman CSB

Do not lack diligence; be fervent in spirit; serve the Lord.

Romans 12:11 Holman CSB

So roll up your sleeves, put your mind in gear, be totally ready to receive the gift that's coming when Jesus arrives. Don't lazily slip back into those old grooves of evil, doing just what you feel like doing. You didn't know any better then; you do now. As obedient children, let yourselves be pulled into a way of life shaped by God's life, a life energetic and blazing with holiness.

1 Peter 1:13-15 MSG

MY PRIORITIES FOR LIFE

I understand the importance of striving to live a life of purpose and passion.

I will share my efforts—and my enthusiasm—with my family, with my friends, and with the world.

I will strive to find activities that I can support wholeheartedly and enthusiastically.

Check Your Priority		
High	Med.	Low
—	—	—
—	—	—
—	—	—

Actions Speak Louder

We have around us many people whose lives tell us what faith means.
So let us run the race that is before us and never give up.
We should remove from our lives anything that would
get in the way and the sin that so easily holds us back.

Hebrews 12:1 NCV

What kind of example are you? Are you the kind of man whose life serves as a genuine example of righteousness? Does your behavior serve as a positive role model for others? Are you the kind of believer whose actions, day in and day out, are based upon kindness, faithfulness, and a love for the Lord? If so, you are not only blessed by God, you are also a powerful force for good in a world that desperately needs positive influences such as yours.

Phillips Brooks had simple advice for believers of every generation; he said, "Be such a person, and live such a life, that if every person were such as you, and every life a life like yours, this earth would be God's Paradise." And that's precisely the kind of Christian you should strive to be . . . but it isn't always easy.

You live in a dangerous, temptation-filled world. That's why you encounter so many opportunities to stray from God's commandments. Resist those temptations! When you do, you'll earn God's blessings, and you'll serve as a positive role model for your family and friends.

Corrie ten Boom advised, "Don't worry about what you do not understand. Worry about what you do understand in the Bible but do not live by." And that's sound advice because your families and friends are watching . . . and so, for that matter, is God.

In our faith we follow in someone's steps.
In our faith we leave footprints to guide others.
It's the principle of discipleship.

Max Lucado

You are the light that gives light to the world.
In the same way, you should be a light for other people.
Live so that they will see the good things you do
and will praise your Father in heaven.

Matthew 5:14,16 NCV

PRIORITIES FOR MY LIFE

Your life is a sermon . . . What kind of sermon will you preach? The words you choose to speak may have some impact on others, but not nearly as much impact as the life you choose to live.

TIMELESS WISDOM FOR GODLY LIVING

You can never separate a leader's actions from his character.

John Maxwell

We urgently need people who encourage and inspire us to move toward God and away from the world's enticing pleasures.

Jim Cymbala

For one man who can introduce another to Jesus Christ by the way he lives and by the atmosphere of his life, there are a thousand who can only talk jargon about him.

Oswald Chambers

A person who lives right and is right has more power in his silence than another has by words.

Phillips Brooks

In every way be an example of doing good deeds. When you teach, do it with honesty and seriousness.
Titus 2:7 NCV

We can talk about faith, but what we live shows the true faith behind the words.

Jay Kesler

MORE WORDS FROM GOD'S WORD

In everything you do, stay away from complaining and arguing, so that no one can speak a word of blame against you. You are to live clean, innocent lives as children of God in a dark world full of crooked and perverse people. Let your lives shine brightly before them.

Philippians 2:14-15 NLT

Do you want to be counted wise, to build a reputation for wisdom? Here's what you do: Live well, live wisely, live humbly. It's the way you live, not the way you talk, that counts.

James 3:13 MSG

You should be an example to the believers in speech, in conduct, in love, in faith, in purity.

1 Timothy 4:12 Holman CSB

MY PRIORITIES FOR LIFE

	Check Your Priority	
High	Med.	Low

I value the importance of setting a good example.

— — —

I understand that my behavior speaks volumes about my relationship with God.

— — —

I understand that I am a role model to my family and friends, and I behave accordingly.

— — —

Joyful Living

Let the hearts of those who seek the Lord rejoice.
Look to the Lord and his strength; seek his face always.

1 Chronicles 16:10-11 NIV

Have you made the choice to rejoice? If you're a Christian, you have every reason to be joyful. After all, the ultimate battle has already been won on the cross at Calvary. And if your life has been transformed by Christ's sacrifice, then you, as a recipient of God's grace, have every reason to live joyfully. Yet sometimes, amid the inevitable hustle and bustle of life-here-on-earth, you may lose sight of your blessings as you wrestle with the challenges of everyday life.

Do you seek happiness, abundance, and contentment? If so, here are some things you should do: Love God and His Son; depend upon God for strength; try, to the best of your abilities, to follow God's will; and strive to obey His Holy Word. When you do these things, you'll discover that happiness goes hand-in-hand with righteousness. The happiest people are not those who rebel against God; the happiest people are those who love God and obey His commandments.

What does life have in store for you? A world full of possibilities (of course it's up to you to accept it). So, as you embark upon the next phase of your journey, remember to celebrate the life that God has given you. Your Creator has blessed you beyond measure. Honor Him with your prayers, your words, your deeds, and your joy.

Joy comes not from what we have but from what we are.

C. H. Spurgeon

The Word of Life appeared right before our eyes; we saw it happen! And now we're telling you in most sober prose that what we witnessed was, incredibly, this: The infinite Life of God himself took shape before us. We saw it, we heard it, and now we're telling you so you can experience it along with us, this experience of communion with the Father and his Son, Jesus Christ. Our motive for writing is simply this: We want you to enjoy this, too. Your joy will double our joy!

1 John 1:2-4 MSG

PRIORITIES FOR MY LIFE

Joy begins with a choice—the choice to establish a genuine relationship with God and His Son.

TIMELESS WISDOM FOR GODLY LIVING

Joy is the serious business of heaven.

C. S. Lewis

Joy has nothing to do with circumstances. Joy is a choice. It is a matter of attitude that stems from one's confidence in God.

Charles Swindoll

Rejoice, the Lord is King; Your Lord and King adore! Rejoice, give thanks and sing and triumph evermore.

Charles Wesley

True happiness and contentment cannot come from the things of this world. The blessedness of true joy is a free gift that comes only from our Lord and Savior, Jesus Christ.

Dennis Swanberg

A joyful heart is good medicine,
but a broken spirit dries up the bones.
Proverbs 17:22 NASB

Joy can be the echo of God's life within you.

Duane Pederson

MORE WORDS FROM GOD'S WORD

Rejoice evermore. Pray without ceasing. In every thing give thanks: for this is the will of God in Christ Jesus concerning you.

1 Thessalonians 5:16-18 KJV

These things I have spoken to you, that My joy may remain in you, and that your joy may be full.

John 15:11 NKJV

Always be full of joy in the Lord. I say it again—rejoice!

Philippians 4:4 NLT

Rejoice, and be exceeding glad: for great is your reward in heaven . . . .

Matthew 5:12 KJV

MY PRIORITIES FOR LIFE

I understand that every day can and should be a cause for celebration.

I will strive to worry less and trust God more.

I will share my enthusiasm with my family, with my friends, and with the world.

Check Your Priority		
High	Med.	Low
—	—	—
—	—	—
—	—	—

The Wisdom To Be Thankful

*In everything give thanks; for this is the will of God
in Christ Jesus for you.*

1 Thessalonians 5:18 NKJV

As believers who have been touched by God's grace, we are blessed beyond measure. God sent His only Son to die for our sins. And, God has given us the priceless gifts of eternal love and eternal life. We, in turn, are instructed to approach our Heavenly Father with reverence and thanksgiving. But, as busy people caught up in the inevitable demands of everyday life, we sometimes fail to pause and thank our Creator for the countless blessings that He has bestowed upon us.

Sometimes life is complicated; sometimes life is frustrating; and sometimes life is downright exhausting. When the demands of life leave us rushing from place to place with scarcely a moment to spare, we may fail to pause and thank our Creator for His gifts. Yet whenever we neglect to give proper thanks to the Giver of all things good, we suffer because of our misplaced priorities.

The words of 1 Thessalonians 5:18 remind us to give thanks in every circumstance of life: "In everything give thanks; for this is the will of God in Christ Jesus for you" (NKJV). But sometimes, when our hearts are troubled and our lives seem to be spinning out of control, we don't feel like thanking anybody, including our Father in heaven. Yet God's Word is clear: In all circumstances, our Creator offers us His love, His strength, and His Grace. And in all circumstances, we must thank Him.

Thoughtful believers (like you) see the need to praise God with sincerity, with humility, and with consistency. So whatever your circumstances—even if you are overworked, over-committed, and overstressed—slow down and express your thanks to the Creator. When you do, you'll discover that your expressions of gratitude will enrich your own life as well as the lives of your loved ones.

Thanksgiving should become a habit, a regular part of your daily routine. After all, God has blessed you beyond measure, and you owe Him everything, including your eternal gratitude . . . starting now.

The game was to just find something about everything to be glad about—no matter what it was. You see, when you're hunting for the glad things, you sort of forget the other kind.

Eleanor H. Porter

PRIORITIES FOR MY LIFE

Two Magic Words: Thank you! People never become tired of hearing those two little words, and neither, for that matter, does God.

TIMELESS WISDOM FOR GODLY LIVING

When it comes to life, the critical thing is whether you take things for granted or take them with gratitude.

G. K. Chesterton

Thanksgiving or complaining—these words express two contrastive attitudes of the souls of God's children in regard to His dealings with them. The soul that gives thanks can find comfort in everything; the soul that complains can find comfort in nothing.

Hannah Whitall Smith

Grace and gratitude belong together like heaven and earth. Grace evokes gratitude like the voice of an echo. Gratitude follows grace as thunder follows lightning.

Karl Barth

Our prayers for you are always spilling over into thanksgivings. We can't quit thanking God our Father and Jesus our Messiah for you!
Colossians 1:3 MSG

Thank God every morning when you get up that you have something to do that day which must be done, whether you like it or not.

Charles Kingsley

MORE WORDS FROM GOD'S WORD

Finally, brethren, whatsoever things are true, whatsoever things are honest, whatsoever things are just, whatsoever things are pure, whatsoever things are lovely, whatsoever things are of good report; if there be any virtue, and if there be any praise, think on these things.

Philippians 4:8 KJV

Enter his gates with thanksgiving, go into his courts with praise. Give thanks to him and bless his name.

Psalm 100:4 NLT

O come, let us sing unto the LORD: let us make a joyful noise to the rock of our salvation. Let us come before his presence with thanksgiving, and make a joyful noise unto him with psalms.

Psalm 95:1-2 KJV

MY PRIORITIES FOR LIFE

| | Check Your Priority | |
High	Med.	Low

I will not take my blessings for granted.

| — | — | — |

I will remain humble as I praise God and thank Him for His gifts.

| — | — | — |

I will not only thank God for His gifts, I will use those gifts as one way of honoring Him.

| — | — | — |

I will expect God's continued blessings on me and my family.

| — | — | — |

The Right Kind of Fear

Honor all people. Love the brotherhood. Fear God. Honor the king.

1 Peter 2:17 NKJV

Are you a Christian who possesses a healthy, fearful respect for God's power? Hopefully so. After all, God's Word teaches that the fear of the Lord is the beginning of knowledge (Proverbs 1:7).

When you fear the Creator—and when you honor Him by obeying His commandments—you will receive God's approval and His blessings. But, if you ignore Him or disobey His commandments, you invite disastrous consequences.

God's hand shapes the universe, and it shapes our lives. God maintains absolute sovereignty over His creation, and His power is beyond comprehension. As believers, we must cultivate a sincere respect for God's awesome power. The fear of the Lord is, indeed, the surest form of wisdom.

In the book of Exodus, God warns that we should place no gods before Him. Yet all too often, we place our Lord in second, third, or fourth place as we worship the gods of pride, greed, power, or lust.

When we place our desires for material possessions above our love for God—or when we yield to temptations of the flesh—

we find ourselves engaged in a struggle that is similar to the one Jesus faced when He was tempted by Satan. In the wilderness, Satan offered Jesus earthly power and unimaginable riches, but Jesus turned Satan away and chose instead to worship God. We must seek to imitate Christ by putting God first and worshiping only Him.

Is God your top priority? Have you given His Son your heart, your soul, your talents, and your time? Or are you in the habit of giving God little more than a few hours on Sunday morning? The answer to these questions will determine how you prioritize your days and your life.

So today, as you face the realities of everyday life, remember this: until you acquire a healthy fear of God's power, your education is incomplete, and so is your faith.

If we do not tremble before God, the world's system seems wonderful to us and pleasantly consumes us.

James Montgomery Boice

PRIORITIES FOR MY LIFE

It's the right kind of fear. Your respect for God should make you fearful of disobeying Him . . . very fearful.

TIMELESS WISDOM FOR GODLY LIVING

The remarkable thing about fearing God is that when you fear God, you fear nothing else, whereas if you do not fear God, you fear everything else.

Oswald Chambers

Remember that this fear of the Lord is His treasure, a choice jewel, given only to favorites, and to those who are greatly beloved.

John Bunyan

A healthy fear of God will do much to deter us from sin.

Charles Swindoll

It is not possible that mortal men should be thoroughly conscious of the divine presence without being filled with awe.

C. H. Spurgeon

Fear the LORD your God,
serve him only and take your oaths in his name.
Deuteronomy 6:13 NIV

When true believers are awed by the greatness of God and by the privilege of becoming His children, then they become sincerely motivated, effective evangelists.

Bill Hybels

MORE WORDS FROM GOD'S WORD

The fear of the Lord is the beginning of knowledge, but fools despise wisdom and discipline.

Proverbs 1:7 NIV

The fear of the Lord is a fountain of life . . . .

Proverbs 14:27 NIV

How blessed is everyone who fears the LORD, who walks in His ways.

Psalm 128:1 NASB

Brothers, sons of Abraham's race, and those among you who fear God, the message of this salvation has been sent to us.

Acts 13:26 Holman CSB

Don't consider yourself to be wise; fear the Lord and turn away from evil.

Proverbs 3:7 Holman CSB

MY PRIORITIES FOR LIFE

I believe that it is important to have a healthy respect for God's power.

I have a healthy fear of disobeying God.

I think that it is important to find ways to worship God throughout the day.

Check Your Priority		
High	Med.	Low
—	—	—
—	—	—
—	—	—

The Joys of Friendship

A friend loves you all the time,
and a brother helps in time of trouble.

Proverbs 17:17 NCV

The dictionary defines the word friend as "a person who is attached to another by feelings of affection or personal regard." This definition is accurate, as far as it goes, but when we examine the deeper meaning of friendship, many more descriptors come to mind: trustworthiness, loyalty, helpfulness, kindness, understanding, forgiveness, encouragement, humor, and cheerfulness, to mention but a few. Needless to say, our trusted friends and family members can help us discover God's unfolding priorities for our lives. Our task is to enlist our friends' wisdom, their cooperation, their honesty, and their encouragement.

An old familiar hymn begins, "What a friend we have in Jesus...." No truer words were ever penned. Jesus is the sovereign friend and ultimate Savior of mankind. Just as Christ has been—and will always be—the ultimate friend to His flock, so should we be Christ-like in our love and devotion to our own little flock of friends and neighbors. When we share the love of Christ, we share a priceless gift. As loyal friends, we must do no less.

As you consider the many blessings that God has given you, remember to thank Him for the friends He has chosen to place along your path. Seek their guidance, and, when asked, never withhold yours. Then, as you travel through life with trusted companions by your side, you will bless them, and they will richly bless you.

Loyal Christian friendship is ordained by God. Throughout the Bible, we are reminded to love one another, to care for one another, and to treat one another as we wish to be treated. So remember the important role that Christian friendship plays in God's plans for His kingdom and for your life. Resolve to be a trustworthy, loyal friend. And, treasure the people in your life who are loyal friends to you. Friendship is, after all, a glorious gift, praised by God. Give thanks for that gift and nurture it.

A true friend is the gift of God,
and He only who made hearts can unite them.

Robert South

PRIORITIES FOR MY LIFE

Remember the first rule of friendship: it's the Golden one, and it starts like this: "Do unto others . . ." (Matthew 7:12)

TIMELESS WISDOM FOR GODLY LIVING

No man can be happy without a friend nor be sure of his friend till he is unhappy.

Thomas Fuller

We have the Lord, but he Himself has recognized that we need the touch of a human hand. He Himself came down and lived among us as a man. We cannot see Him now, but blessed be the tie that binds human hearts in Christian love.

Vance Havner

The friend who can be silent with us in a moment of despair or confusion, who can stay with us in an hour of grief and bereavement, who can tolerate not-knowing, not-curing, not-healing and face with us the reality of our powerlessness, that is the friend who cares.

Henri Nouwen

> Greater love has no one than this,
> that he lay down his life for his friends.
> John 15:13 NIV

A friend is long sought, hardly found and with difficulty kept.

St. Jerome

MORE WORDS FROM GOD'S WORD

If a fellow believer hurts you, go and tell him—work it out between the two of you. If he listens, you've made a friend.

Matthew 18:15 MSG

Beloved, if God so loved us, we also ought to love one another.

1 John 4:11 NKJV

I thank my God upon every remembrance of you.

Philippians 1:3 NKJV

Iron sharpeneth iron; so a man sharpeneth the countenance of his friend.

Proverbs 27:17 KJV

MY PRIORITIES FOR LIFE

I believe that it is important to make friends and to keep friends.

Check Your Priority		
High	Med.	Low
—	—	—

In building friendships, I emphasize the need for mutual honesty and mutual trust.

—	—	—

Because I want to cultivate my friendships, I make the effort to spend time with my friends.

—	—	—

Mountain-moving Faith

Be on the alert, stand firm in the faith,
act like men, be strong.

1 Corinthians 16:13 NASB

Every life (including yours) can be a grand adventure in faithful living . . . or not. And, every day (including this one) presents the opportunity to trust God faithfully . . . or to ignore Him altogether. The decision to trust God is yours, and so are the consequences of that decision.

Your life, like every life, is a series of successes and failures, celebrations and disappointments, joys and sorrows. Every step of the way, through every triumph and tragedy, God will stand by your side and strengthen you . . . if you have faith in Him. Jesus taught His disciples that if they had faith, they could move mountains. You can too.

How can you strengthen your faith? Through praise, through worship, through Bible study, and through prayer. And, as your faith becomes stronger, you will find ways to share it with your friends, your family, and with the world. When you place your faith, your trust, indeed your life in the hands of Christ Jesus, you'll be amazed at the marvelous things He can do with you and through you; so trust God's plans. With Him, all things are possible, and He stands ready to open a world of possibilities to you . . . if you have faith.

Today, you may face challenges that leave you discouraged or exhausted. If so, remember this: whatever your challenge, whatever your trouble, God can handle it. And will. Just place your faith in Him, and then, with no further ado, let the mountain-moving begin.

Where reason cannot wade, there faith must swim.

Thomas Watson

Fight the good fight of faith;
take hold of the eternal life to which you were called . . . .

1 Timothy 6:12 NASB

PRIORITIES FOR MY LIFE

Faith should be practiced more than studied. Vance Havner said, "Nothing is more disastrous than to study faith, analyze faith, make noble resolves of faith, but never actually to make the leap of faith." How true!

TIMELESS WISDOM FOR GODLY LIVING

God doesn't always change the circumstances, but He can change us to meet the circumstances. That's what it means to live by faith.

Warren Wiersbe

Great hopes make great men.

Thomas Fuller

Faith is not an easy virtue; but, in the broad world of man's total voyage through time to eternity, faith is not only a gracious companion, but an essential guide.

Theodore Hesburgh

True faith must always be measured by self-despair; or in other words, the measure of your trust in Christ must be the measure of your distrust in self.

Stephen Olford

> *For whatever is born of God overcomes the world.*
> *And this is the victory that has*
> *overcome the world—our faith.*
> 1 John 5:4 NKJV

Faith is blind—except upward. It is blind to impossibilities, and deaf to doubt. It listens only to God and sees only his power and acts accordingly.

S. D. Gordon

MORE WORDS FROM GOD'S WORD

Therefore, being always of good courage . . . we walk by faith, not by sight.

2 Corinthians 5:6-7 NASB

I have fought the good fight, I have finished the race, I have kept the faith.

2 Timothy 4:7 NIV

It is impossible to please God apart from faith. And why? Because anyone who wants to approach God must believe both that he exists and that he cares enough to respond to those who seek him.

Hebrews 11:6 MSG

Anything is possible if a person believes.

Mark 9:23 NLT

MY PRIORITIES FOR LIFE

| | Check Your Priority | |
High	Med.	Low

I believe in the power of faith to "make me whole."

— — —

My faith is stronger when I keep my eyes on Jesus and not on my circumstances.

— — —

I believe that faith is a choice, and I choose to have faith.

— — —

Sharing
Your Testimony

But the following night the Lord stood by him and said,
"Be of good cheer, Paul; for as you have testified for Me."

Acts 23:11 NKJV

Have you made the decision to allow Christ to reign over your heart? If so, you have an important story to tell: yours.

Your personal testimony is profoundly important, but perhaps because of shyness (or because of the fear of being rebuffed), you've been hesitant to share your experiences. If so, you should start paying less attention to your own insecurities and more attention to the message that God wants you to share with the world.

In his second letter to Timothy, Paul shares a message to believers of every generation when he writes, "God has not given us a spirit of timidity" (1:7 NASB). Paul's meaning is clear: When sharing our testimonies, we must be courageous, forthright, and unashamed.

Corrie ten Boom observed, "There is nothing anybody else can do that can stop God from using us. We can turn everything into a testimony." Her words remind us that when we speak up for God, our actions may speak even more loudly than our words.

When we let other people know the details of our faith, we assume an important responsibility: the responsibility of making certain that our words are reinforced by our actions. When we share our testimonies, we must also be willing to serve as shining examples of righteousness—undeniable examples of the changes that Jesus makes in the lives of those who accept Him as their Savior.

Are you willing to follow in the footsteps of Jesus? If so, you must also be willing to talk about Him. And make no mistake—the time to express your belief in Him is now. You know how He has touched your own heart; help Him do the same for others.

There is a glorified Man on the right hand of the Majesty
in heaven faithfully representing us there.
We are left for a season among men;
let us faithfully represent Him here.

A. W. Tozer

PRIORITIES FOR MY LIFE

Your story is important: D. L. Moody, the famed evangelist from Chicago, said, "Remember, a small light will do a great deal when it is in a very dark place. Put one little tallow candle in the middle of a large hall, and it will give a great deal of light." Make certain that your candle is always lit. Give your testimony, and trust God to do the rest.

TIMELESS WISDOM FOR GODLY LIVING

Every believer may be brought to understand that the only object of his life is to help to make Christ King on the earth.

Andrew Murray

The sermon of your life in tough times ministers to people more powerfully than the most eloquent speaker.

Bill Bright

To stand in an uncaring world and say, "See, here is the Christ" is a daring act of courage.

Calvin Miller

We need to talk to God about people, then talk to people about God.

Dieter Zander

> *But respect Christ as the holy Lord in your hearts. Always be ready to answer everyone who asks you to explain about the hope you have.*
> 1 Peter 3:15 NCV

How many people have you made homesick for God?

Oswald Chambers

MORE WORDS FROM GOD'S WORD

This and this only has been my appointed work: getting this news to those who have never heard of God, and explaining how it works by simple faith and plain truth.

1 Timothy 2:7 MSG

For God has not given us a spirit of fear and timidity, but of power, love, and self-discipline. So you must never be ashamed to tell others about our Lord.

2 Timothy 1:7-8 NLT

The following night, the Lord stood by him and said, "Have courage! For as you have testified about Me in Jerusalem, so you must also testify in Rome."

Acts 23:11 Holman CSB

MY PRIORITIES FOR LIFE

	Check Your Priority	
	High	Med.	Low

I understand the importance of sharing my personal testimony.

— — —

I understand the importance of making certain that my actions are consistent with my words.

— — —

I believe that every day presents another opportunity to share Christ's message with my family, with my friends, and with the world.

— — —

Behavior That Pleases God

Light shines on the godly, and joy on those who do right.
May all who are godly be happy in the Lord and praise his holy name.

Psalm 97:11-12 NLT

If you're like most people, you seek the admiration of your neighbors, your coworkers, and your family members. But the eagerness to please others should never overshadow your eagerness to please God. If you seek to fulfill the purposes that God has in store for you, then you must be a "doer of the Word." And how can you do so? By putting God first.

The words of Matthew 6:33 make it clear: "But seek first the kingdom of God and His righteousness, and all these things will be provided for you" (Holman CSB). God has given you a priceless guidebook, an indispensable tool for "seeking His kingdom." That tool, of course, is the Holy Bible. It contains thorough instructions which, if followed, lead to fulfillment, righteousness and salvation.

But for those who would ignore God's Word, Martin Luther issued this stern warning: "You may as well quit reading and hearing the Word of God and give it to the devil if you do not desire to live according to it." Luther understood that obedience leads to abundance just as surely as disobedience leads to disaster; you should understand it, too.

Each new day presents countless opportunities to put God in first place . . . or not. When you honor Him by living according to His commandments, you earn the abundance and peace that He promises. But, if you ignore God's teachings, you will inevitably bring needless suffering upon yourself and your family.

Would you like a time-tested formula for successful living? Here it is: Don't just listen to God's Word, live by it. Does this sound too simple? Perhaps it is simple, but it is also the only way to reap the marvelous riches that God has in store for you.

I don't care what a man says he believes with his lips.
I want to know with a vengeance what
he says with his life and his actions.

Sam Jones

PRIORITIES FOR MY LIFE

When it comes to telling the world about your relationship with God, your actions speak much more loudly than your words . . . so behave yourself accordingly.

TIMELESS WISDOM FOR GODLY LIVING

Preach the gospel at all times and, if necessary, use words.

St. Francis of Assisi

True moral freedom is the ability to live according to God's purposes.

Stanley Grenz

Conviction is worthless until it is converted into conduct.

Thomas Carlyle

God meant that we adjust to the Gospel—not the other way around.

Vance Havner

Even a child is known by his actions,
by whether his conduct is pure and right.
Proverbs 20:11 NIV

Christians are the citizens of heaven, and while we are on earth, we ought to behave like heaven's citizens.

Warren Wiersbe

MORE WORDS FROM GOD'S WORD

Therefore by their fruits you will know them.

Matthew 7:20 NKJV

He who has My commandments and keeps them, it is he who loves Me. And he who loves Me will be loved by My Father, and I will love him and manifest Myself to him.

John 14:21 NKJV

Who is wise and understanding among you? Let him show by good conduct that his works are done in the meekness of wisdom.

James 3:13 NKJV

Light shines on the godly, and joy on those who do right. May all who are godly be happy in the Lord and praise his holy name.

Psalm 97:11-12 NLT

MY PRIORITIES FOR LIFE

I understand that my behavior reveals my relationship with God.

I understand that my behavior affects how I feel about myself.

I know that my behavior should reflect Biblical values.

Check Your Priority		
High	Med.	Low
—	—	—
—	—	—
—	—	—

The Right Kind of Attitude

Set your mind on things above, not on things on the earth.

Colossians 3:2 NKJV

Of course you've heard the saying, "Life is what you make it." And although that statement may seem very trite, it's also very true. You can choose a life filled to the brim with frustration and fear, or you can choose a life of abundance and peace. That choice is up to you—and only you—and it depends, to a surprising extent, upon your attitude.

What's your attitude today? Are you fearful, angry, bored, or worried? Are you pessimistic, perplexed, pained, and perturbed? Are you moping around with a frown on your face that's almost as big as the one in your heart? If so, God wants to have a little talk with you.

God created you in His own image, and He wants you to experience joy, contentment, peace, and abundance. But, God will not force you to experience these things; you must claim them for yourself.

God has given you free will, including the ability to influence the direction and the tone of your thoughts. And, here's how God wants you to direct those thoughts:

"Finally brothers, whatever is true, whatever is honorable, whatever is just, whatever is pure, whatever is lovely, whatever is commendable—if there is any moral excellence and if there is any praise—dwell on these things" (Philippians 4:8 Holman CSB).

The quality of your attitude will help determine the quality of your life, so you must guard your thoughts accordingly. If you make up your mind to approach life with a healthy mixture of realism and optimism, you'll be rewarded. But, if you allow yourself to fall into the unfortunate habit of negative thinking, you will doom yourself to unhappiness, or mediocrity, or worse.

So, the next time you find yourself dwelling upon the negative aspects of your life, refocus your attention on positive things. The next time you find yourself falling prey to the blight of pessimism, stop yourself and turn your thoughts around. The next time you're tempted to waste valuable time gossiping or complaining, resist those temptations with all your might.

And remember: You'll never whine your way to the top . . . so don't waste your breath.

The purity of motive determines the quality of action.

Oswald Chambers

PRIORITIES FOR MY LIFE

Learn about Jesus and His attitude. Then try and do what Jesus would do.

TIMELESS WISDOM FOR GODLY LIVING

It's your choice: you can either count your blessings or recount your disappointments.

Jim Gallery

First thing every morning before you arise, say out loud, "I believe," three times.

Norman Vincent Peale

Do you feel the world is treating you well? If your attitude toward the world is excellent, you will receive excellent results. If you feel so-so about the world, your response from that world will be average. If you feel badly about your world, you will seem to have only negative feedback from life.

John Maxwell

Come near to God, and God will come near to you.
You sinners, clean sin out of your lives.
You who are trying to follow God and the world
at the same time, make your thinking pure.
James 4:8 NCV

The last of the human freedoms is to choose one's attitude in any given set of circumstances.

Viktor Frankl

MORE WORDS FROM GOD'S WORD

Those who are pure in their thinking are happy, because they will be with God.

Matthew 5:8 NCV

So prepare your minds for service and have self-control.

1 Peter 1:13 NCV

For God has not given us a spirit of fear, but of power and of love and of a sound mind.

2 Timothy 1:7 NLT

Keep your eyes focused on what is right, and look straight ahead to what is good.

Proverbs 4:25 NCV

MY PRIORITIES FOR LIFE

I believe that if I want to change certain aspects of my life, I also need to make adjustments in my own attitudes toward life.

I believe that it is important to associate myself with people who are upbeat, optimistic, and encouraging.

I believe that it is important to focus my thoughts on the positive aspects of life, not the negative ones.

Check Your Priority

High   Med.   Low

—   —   —

—   —   —

—   —   —

Celebrating Life

Celebrate God all day, every day. I mean, revel in him!

Philippians 4:4 MSG

Today is a non-renewable resource—once it's gone, it's gone forever. Our responsibility, as thoughtful believers, is to use this day in the service of God's will and in the service of His people. When we do so, we enrich our own lives and the lives of those whom we love.

God has richly blessed us, and He wants you to rejoice in His gifts. That's why this day—and each day that follows—should be a time of prayer and celebration as we consider the Good News of God's free gift: salvation through Jesus Christ.

Oswald Chambers correctly observed, "Joy is the great note all throughout the Bible." E. Stanley Jones echoed that thought when he wrote "Christ and joy go together." But, even the most dedicated Christians can, on occasion, forget to celebrate each day for what it is: a priceless gift from God.

What do you expect from the day ahead? Are you expecting God to do wonderful things, or are you living beneath a cloud of apprehension and doubt? The familiar words of Psalm 118:24 remind us of a profound yet simple truth: "This is the day which the LORD hath made" (KJV). Our duty, as believers, is to rejoice in God's marvelous creation.

Today, celebrate the life that God has given you. Today, put a smile on your face, kind words on your lips, and a song in your heart. Be generous with your praise and free with your encouragement. And then, when you have celebrated life to the fullest, invite your friends to do likewise. After all, this is God's day, and He has given us clear instructions for its use. We are commanded to rejoice and be glad. So, with no further ado, let the celebration begin . . .

Celebration is possible only through the deep realization that life and death are never found completely separate. Celebration can really come about only where fear and love, joy and sorrow, tear and smiles can exist together.

Henri Nouwen

PRIORITIES FOR MY LIFE

If you're feeling down, perhaps all you need is an attitude adjustment: if so, start focusing more on the donut and less on the hole. But if you're feeling really sad or deeply depressed, TALKING ABOUT IT with people can help. Then, don't hesitate to speak with your doctor, or your pastor, or better yet, with both. Help is available. Ask for it. NOW!

TIMELESS WISDOM FOR GODLY LIVING

The church is the last place on earth to be solemn . . . provided you have lived right.

Sam Jones

All our life is a celebration for us; we are convinced, in fact, that God is always everywhere. We sing while we work . . . we pray while we carry out all life's other occupations.

St. Clement of Alexandria

I know nothing, except what everyone knows—if there when God dances, I should dance.

W. H. Auden

David and the whole house of Israel were celebrating with all their might before the LORD, with songs and with harps, lyres, tambourines, sistrums and cymbals.
2 Samuel 6:5 NIV

If you can forgive the person you were, accept the person you are, and believe in the person you will become, you are headed for joy. So celebrate your life.

Barbara Johnson

MORE WORDS FROM GOD'S WORD

At the dedication of the wall of Jerusalem, the Levites were sought out from where they lived and were brought to Jerusalem to celebrate joyfully the dedication with songs of thanksgiving and with the music of cymbals, harps and lyres.

Nehemiah 12:27 NIV

A happy heart is like a continual feast.

Proverbs 15:15 NCV

Shout for joy to the LORD, all the earth. Worship the LORD with gladness; come before him with joyful songs.

Psalm 100:1-2 NIV

So now we can rejoice in our wonderful new relationship with God—all because of what our Lord Jesus Christ has done for us in making us friends of God.

Romans 5:11 NLT

MY PRIORITIES FOR LIFE

| | Check Your Priority | |
High	Med.	Low

I understand the need to celebrate God's gifts.

— — —

I will celebrate God's gifts with my family
and friends.

— — —

I will consider each new day a cause for celebration.

— — —

Tackling Tough Times

*We also have joy with our troubles, because we know that
these troubles produce patience. And patience produces character,
and character produces hope.*

Romans 5:3-4 NCV

As life unfolds, all of us encounter occasional setbacks: Those periodic visits from Old Man Trouble are simply a fact of life, and none of us are exempt. When tough times arrive, we may be forced to rearrange our plans but we must never rearrange our values.

The fact that we encounter adversity is not nearly so important as the way we choose to deal with it. When tough times arrive, we have a clear choice: we can begin the difficult work of tackling our troubles . . . or not. When we summon the courage to look Old Man Trouble squarely in the eye, he usually blinks. But, if we refuse to address our problems, even the smallest annoyances have a way of growing into king-sized catastrophes.

Psalm 145 promises, "The Lord is near to all who call on him, to all who call on him in truth. He fulfills the desires of those who fear him; he hears their cry and saves them." (v. 18-20 NIV). And the words of Jesus offer us comfort: I tell you the truth, you will weep and mourn while the world rejoices. You will grieve, but your grief will turn to joy" (John 16:20 NIV).

As believers, we know that God loves us and that He will protect us. In times of hardship, He will comfort us; in times of sorrow, He will dry our tears. When we are troubled, or weak, or sorrowful, God is always with us. We must build our lives on the rock that cannot be shaken: we must trust in God. And then, we must get on with the hard work of tackling our problems . . . because if we don't, who will? Or should?

Never fancy you could be something if only you had a different lot and sphere assigned to you. The very things that you most denounce as fatal limitations or obstructions, are probably what you most want. What you call hindrances, obstacles, discouragements, are probably God's opportunities.

Horace Bushnell

PRIORITIES FOR MY LIFE

Tough Times 101: Sometimes, when we encounter tough times, we find ourselves "starting over." From scratch. As believers we can find comfort in the knowledge that wherever we find ourselves, whether on the mountaintops of life or in the deepest valleys of despair, God is there with us. And just as importantly, we never have to "start over" with Him, because He never left us!

TIMELESS WISDOM FOR GODLY LIVING

If you are a true believer, and he still puts thorns in your bed, it is only to keep you from falling into the somnolence of complacency; it is to ensure that you "continue in His goodness" by letting your sense of need bring you back constantly in faith to seek His face.

J. I. Packer

One's attitude toward a handicap determines its impact on his life.

James Dobson

Trouble is one of God's great servants because it reminds us how much we continually need the Lord.

Jim Cymbala

Afflictions make the heart more deep, more knowing, and more profound.

John Bunyan

The LORD also will be a stronghold for the oppressed, a stronghold in times of trouble.

Psalm 9:9 NASB

The only way to learn a strong faith is to endure great trials. I have learned my faith by standing firm amid the most severe of tests.

George Mueller

MORE WORDS FROM GOD'S WORD

You pulled me from the brink of death, my feet from the cliff-edge of doom. Now I stroll at leisure with God in the sunlit fields of life.

Psalm 56:13 MSG

Come to Me, all you who labor and are heavy laden, and I will give you rest. Take My yoke upon you and learn from Me, for I am gentle and lowly in heart, and you will find rest for your souls. For My yoke is easy and My burden is light.

Matthew 11:28-30 NKJV

The Lord lifts the burdens of those bent beneath their loads. The Lord loves the righteous.

Psalm 146:8 NLT

MY PRIORITIES FOR LIFE

In dealing with difficult situations, I view God as my comfort and my strength.

I believe that difficult times can also be times of intense personal growth.

I understand the importance of comforting others who find themselves in difficult circumstances.

Check Your Priority		
High	Med.	Low
—	—	—
—	—	—
—	—	—

Keeping Money in Perspective

For I am the Lord, I do not change. Will a man rob God?
Yet you have robbed Me! But you say, in what way have we robbed You?
In tithes and offerings. You are cursed with a curse, for you have
robbed Me, even this whole nation. Bring all the tithes into
the storehouse, that there may be food in My house.

Malachi 3:6,8-10 NKJV

Countless books have been written about money—how to make it and how to keep it. But if you're a Christian, you probably already own at least one copy—and probably several copies—of the world's foremost guide to financial security. That book is the Holy Bible. God's Word is not only a road map to eternal life, it is also an indispensable guidebook for life here on earth. As such, the Bible has much to say about your life, your faith, and your finances.

Is the Bible a lamp that guides your path? Is God's Word your everyday guide for every facet of your life (including your finances), or is it a once-a-week text that you consult only on Sunday mornings? Do you read the Bible faithfully or sporadically? The answer to these questions will determine the direction of your thoughts, the direction of your day, and, in many cases, the condition of your financial fortunes.

God's Word reminds us again and again that our Creator expects us to lead disciplined lives. God doesn't reward laziness, misbehavior, or apathy. To the contrary, He expects believers to behave with dignity and discipline . . . but the world tempts us to do otherwise. We live in a world in which leisure is glorified and indifference is often glamorized. But God has other plans. He did not create us for lives of mediocrity; He created us for far greater things.

Life's greatest rewards seldom fall into our laps; to the contrary, our greatest accomplishments (including our financial accomplishments) usually require plenty of work, a heaping helping of wisdom, and a double dose of self discipline—which is perfectly fine with God. After all, He knows that we're up to the task.

God's Word can be a road map to a place of righteous and abundance. Make it your road map. God's wisdom can be a light to guide your steps. Claim it as your light. God's Word can be an invaluable tool for crafting a better day and a better life. Make it your tool. And finally, God's Word can help you organize your financial affairs in such a way that you have less need to worry and more time to celebrate. If that sounds appealing, keep reading this book and God's Book. But not necessarily in that order.

PRIORITIES FOR MY LIFE

Don't fall in love with "stuff." We live in a society that worships "stuff"—don't fall into that trap. Remember this: "stuff" is highly overrated. Worship God Almighty, not the almighty dollar.

TIMELESS WISDOM FOR GODLY LIVING

If your outgo exceeds your income, then your upkeep will be your downfall.

John Maxwell

I sincerely believe that once Christians have been educated in God's plan for their finances, they will find a freedom they had never known before.

Larry Burkett

Discipline understands that the best way to get rich quick is to get rich slow.

Dave Ramsey

A Christian who is not experiencing the peace and fulfillment in financial matters that the Bible promises is in bondage.

Larry Burkett

And my God shall supply all your need according to His riches in glory by Christ Jesus.
Philippians 4:19 NKJV

If you work hard and maintain an attitude of gratitude, you'll find it easier to manage your finances every day.

John Maxwell

MORE WORDS FROM GOD'S WORD

*Honor the Lord with your wealth and the firstfruits from all your crops.
Then your barns will be full, and your wine barrels will overflow with new
wine.*

Proverbs 3:9-10 NCV

*Then she came and told the man of God. And he said, "Go, sell the oil
and pay your debt; and you and your sons live on the rest."*

2 Kings 4:7 NKJV

*Based on the gift they have received, everyone should use it to serve others,
as good managers of the varied grace of God.*

1 Peter 4:10 Holman CSB

MY PRIORITIES FOR LIFE

God is my ultimate financial advisor. I will trust
Him with everything I have.

I understand the importance of being a careful
steward of the money that God has entrusted
to my care.

I will be generous with my tithes and offerings
because I understand that everything I have
ultimately belongs to God.

Check Your Priority		
High	Med.	Low
—	—	—
—	—	—
—	—	—

He Is Here

Come near to God, and God will come near to you.
You sinners, clean sin out of your lives. You who are trying to follow
God and the world at the same time, make your thinking pure.

James 4:8 NCV

In the quiet early morning, as the sun's first rays peak over the horizon, we may sense the presence of God. But as the day wears on and the demands of everyday life bear down upon us, we may become so wrapped up in earthy concerns that we forget to praise the Creator.

God is everywhere we have ever been and everywhere we will ever be. When we turn to Him often, we are blessed by His presence. But, if we ignore God's presence or rebel against it altogether, the world in which we live soon becomes a spiritual wasteland.

Since God is everywhere, we are free to sense His presence whenever we take the time to quiet our souls and turn our prayers to Him. But sometimes, amid the incessant demands of everyday life, we turn our thoughts far from God; when we do, we suffer.

Do you set aside quiet moments each day to offer praise to your Creator? You should. During these moments of stillness, you can sense the infinite love and power of our Lord. The familiar words of Psalm 46:10 remind us to "Be still, and know that I am God" (KJV). When we do so, we encounter the awesome presence of our loving Heavenly Father.

Are you tired, discouraged or fearful? Be comforted because God is with you. Are you confused? Listen to the quiet voice of your Heavenly Father. Are you bitter? Talk with God and seek His guidance. Are you celebrating a great victory? Thank God and praise Him. He is the Giver of all things good. In whatever condition you find yourself—whether you are happy or sad, victorious or vanquished, troubled or triumphant—celebrate God's presence. And be comforted in the knowledge that God is not just near. He is here.

Get yourself into the presence of the loving Father. Just place yourself before Him, and look up into, His face; think of His love, His wonderful, tender, pitying love.

Andrew Murray

PRIORITIES FOR MY LIFE

God is omnipresent meaning He is everywhere. C. S. Lewis observed, "We may ignore, but we can nowhere evade, the presence of God. The world is crowded with Him. He walks everywhere incognito. And the incognito is not always hard to penetrate. The real labour is to remember, to attend. In fact, to come awake. Still more, to remain awake."

TIMELESS WISDOM FOR GODLY LIVING

There is nothing more important in any life than the constantly enjoyed presence of the Lord. There is nothing more vital, for without it we shall make mistakes, and without it we shall be defeated.

Alan Redpath

Because He is spirit, He fills heaven and earth.

Arthur W. Pink

I know that for the right practice, in the presence of God, the heart must be empty of all other things, because God will possess the heart alone; and as He cannot possess it alone without emptying it of all besides, so neither can He act there, and do in it what He pleases, unless it be left vacant to Him.

Brother Lawrence

No, I will not abandon you as orphans—
I will come to you.
John 14:18 NLT

A state of mind that sees God in everything is evidence of growth in grace and of a thankful heart.

Charles Finney

MORE WORDS FROM GOD'S WORD

For the eyes of the Lord range throughout the earth to strengthen those whose hearts are fully committed to him.

2 Chronicles 16:9 NIV

God did this so that men would seek him and perhaps reach out for him and find him, though he is not far from each one of us.

Acts 17:27 NIV

The Lord is near all who call out to Him, all who call out to Him with integrity. He fulfills the desires of those who fear Him; He hears their cry for help and saves them.

Psalm 145:18-19 Holman CSB

MY PRIORITIES FOR LIFE

I believe God seeks a close and intimate relationship with me.

I believe that whenever I feel distance from God, that distance is my own doing, not His.

I believe God is near and that He is guiding me as I seek His wisdom.

Check Your Priority		
High	Med.	Low
—	—	—
—	—	—
—	—	—

The Cheerful Giver

*God has given gifts to each of you from his
great variety of spiritual gifts. Manage them well
so that God's generosity can flow through you.*

1 Peter 4:10 NLT

The thread of generosity is woven—completely and inextricably—into the very fabric of Christ's teachings. As He sent His disciples out to heal the sick and spread God's message of salvation, Jesus offered this guiding principle: "Freely you have received, freely give" (Matthew 10:8 NIV). The principle still applies. If we are to be disciples of Christ, we must give freely of our time, our possessions, and our love.

In 2 Corinthians 9, Paul reminds us that when we sow the seeds of generosity, we reap bountiful rewards in accordance with God's plan for our lives. Thus, we are instructed to give cheerfully and without reservation: "But this I say, He which soweth sparingly shall reap also sparingly; and he which soweth bountifully shall reap also bountifully. Every man according as he purposeth in his heart, so let him give; not grudgingly, or of necessity: for God loveth a cheerful giver" (v. 6, 7 KJV).

Are you a cheerful giver? If you intend to obey God's commandments, you must be. When you give, God looks not only at the quality of your gift, but also at the condition of your heart. If you give generously, joyfully, and without complaint, you obey God's Word. But, if you make your gifts grudgingly, or if the motivation for your gift is selfish, you invite God's displeasure.

One of life's greatest joys is the ability to share your gifts with others. The more you earn and save, the more you'll have to share. So today, make this pledge and keep it: Be a cheerful, generous, courageous giver. The world needs your help, and you need the spiritual rewards that will be yours when you do.

I expect to pass through this life but once. If, therefore,
there be any good thing I can do to any fellow being,
let me do it now, and not defer or neglect it,
as I shall not pass this way again.

William Penn

PRIORITIES FOR MY LIFE

Would you like to be a little happier? Try sharing a few more of the blessings that God has bestowed upon you. In other words, if you want to be happy, be generous. And if you want to be unhappy, be greedy.

TIMELESS WISDOM FOR GODLY LIVING

All the blessings we enjoy are divine deposits, committed to our trust on this condition: that they should be dispensed for the benefit of our neighbors.

John Calvin

Anything done for another is done for oneself.

Pope John Paul II

He climbs highest who helps another up.

Zig Ziglar

Two works of mercy set a man free: forgive and you will be forgiven, and give and you will receive.

St. Augustine

> *Now this I say, he who sows sparingly will also reap sparingly,*
> *and he who sows bountifully will also reap bountifully.*
> *Each one must do just as he has purposed in his heart,*
> *not grudgingly or under compulsion,*
> *for God loves a cheerful giver.*
> 2 Corinthians 9:6-7 NASB

The greatest difficulty with the world is not its ability to produce, but the unwillingness to share.

Roy L. Smith

MORE WORDS FROM GOD'S WORD

Be generous: Invest in acts of charity. Charity yields high returns.

Ecclesiastes 11:1 MSG

Whenever we have the opportunity, we should do good to everyone, especially to our Christian brothers and sisters.

Galatians 6:10 NLT

I tell you the truth, whatever you did for one of the least of these brothers of mine, you did for me.

Matthew 25:40 NIV

The good person is generous and lends lavishly . . . .

Psalm 112:5 MSG

MY PRIORITIES FOR LIFE

	Check Your Priority	
High	Med.	Low

Because I have been blessed by God, it is important for me to share my blessings with others.

— — —

I believe that a direct relationship exists between generosity and joy—the more I give the more joy I experience.

— — —

Jesus Christ gave His life for me; His selfless act motivates me to be a selfless giver.

— — —

The Bread of Life

And Jesus said to them,
"I am the bread of life. He who comes to Me shall
never hunger, and he who believes in Me shall never thirst."

John 6:35 NKJV

He was the Son of God, but He wore a crown of thorns. He was the Savior of mankind, yet He was put to death on a rough-hewn cross. He offered His healing touch to an unsaved world, and yet the same hands that had healed the sick and raised the dead were pierced with nails.

Jesus Christ, the Son of God, was born into humble circumstances. He walked this earth, not as a ruler of men, but as the Savior of mankind. His crucifixion, a torturous punishment that was intended to end His life and His reign, instead became the pivotal event in the history of all humanity. Christ sacrificed His life on the cross so that we might have eternal life. This gift, freely given by God's only begotten Son, is the priceless possession of everyone who accepts Him as Lord and Savior.

Why did Christ endure the humiliation and torture of the cross? He did it for you. His love is as near as your next breath, as personal as your next thought, more essential than your next heartbeat. And what must you do in response to the Savior's gifts? You must accept His love, praise His name, and share His message of salvation. And, you must conduct yourself in a manner that demonstrates to all the world that your acquaintance with the Master is not a passing fancy but that it is, instead, the cornerstone and the touchstone of your life.

O Sovereign God! You have humbled yourself in order to exalt us. You became poor so that we might become rich. You came to us so that we can come to you. You took upon yourself our humanity in order to raise us up into eternal life. All this comes through your grace, free and unmerited; all this through your beloved Son, our Lord and Savior, Jesus Christ.

Karl Barth

PRIORITIES FOR MY LIFE

Let Jesus Make a Real Difference in Your Life: If you're trying to mold your relationship with Jesus into something that fits comfortably into your own schedule and your own personal theology, you may be headed for trouble. A far better strategy is this: conform yourself to Jesus, not vice versa.

TIMELESS WISDOM FOR GODLY LIVING

We accept Jesus Christ, the living Word of God, as our life.

Richard Foster

His name sounds down the corridors of the centuries like the music of all choirs, visible and invisible, poured forth in one anthem.

R. G. Lee

Jesus: the proof of God's love.

Philip Yancey

At the name of Jesus every knee should bow, of those in heaven, and of those on earth, and of those under the earth, and that every tongue should confess that Jesus Christ is Lord, to the glory of God the Father.

Philippians 2:10-11 NKJV

What child is this, Who, laid to rest, on Mary's lap is sleeping? Whom angels greet with anthems sweet, while shepherds watch are keeping? This, this is Christ the King, Whom shepherds guard and angels sing. Haste, haste to bring Him laud, the Babe, the Son of Mary.

William C. Dix

MORE WORDS FROM GOD'S WORD

For I am persuaded, that neither death, nor life, nor angels, nor principalities, nor powers, nor things present, nor things to come, nor height, nor depth, nor any other creature, shall be able to separate us from the love of God, which is in Christ Jesus our Lord.

Romans 8:38-39 KJV

For the Son of Man has come to save that which was lost.

Matthew 18:11 NKJV

Jesus Christ the same yesterday, and today, and for ever.

Hebrews 13:8 KJV

MY PRIORITIES FOR LIFE

	Check Your Priority	
High	Med.	Low

I will accept Jesus as my personal Savior, and I will allow Him to reign over my heart.

— — —

I will share the Good News of Jesus with a world that desperately needs His message.

— — —

I will conduct myself in ways that clearly demonstrate the changes that Christ has made in my life.

— — —

I will make Jesus the cornerstone of my life, and I will honor Him today, tomorrow, and forever.

— — —

Laughing With Life

*There is a time for everything, and a season
for every activity under heaven . . . a time to weep and a time to laugh,
a time to mourn and a time to dance . . . .*

Ecclesiastes 3:1,4 NIV

Laughter is medicine for the soul, but sometimes, amid the stresses of the day, we forget to take our medicine. Instead of viewing our world with a mixture of optimism and humor, we allow worries and distractions to rob us of the joy that God intends for our lives.

So the next time you find yourself dwelling upon the negatives of life, refocus your attention to things positive. The next time you find yourself falling prey to the blight of pessimism, stop yourself and turn your thoughts around. And, if you see your glass as "half-empty," rest assured that your spiritual vision is impaired. With God, your glass is never half empty. With God as your protector and Christ as your Savior, your glass is filled to the brim and overflowing . . . forever.

Today, as you go about your daily activities, approach life with a smile on your lips and hope in your heart. And laugh every chance you get. After all, God created laughter for a reason . . . and Father indeed knows best. So laugh!

When you have good, healthy relationships
with your family and friends you're more prompted
to laugh and not to take yourself so seriously.

Dennis Swanberg

*Shout for joy to the LORD, all the earth, burst into jubilant song
with music; make music to the LORD with the harp,
with the harp and the sound of singing, with trumpets
and the blast of the ram's horn—shout for joy
before the LORD, the King.*

Psalm 98:4-6 NIV

PRIORITIES FOR MY LIFE

Remember: Laughter Is Good Medicine: Milton Berle said, "Laughter is an instant vacation." And when you laugh with your family, it's an instant family vacation.

TIMELESS WISDOM FOR GODLY LIVING

It is pleasing to the dear God whenever you rejoice or laugh from the bottom of your heart.

Martin Luther

If you can laugh at yourself loudly and often, you will find it liberating. There's no better way to prevent stress from becoming distress.

John Maxwell

Laugh and grow strong.

St. Ignatius Loyola

I think everybody ought to be a laughing Christian. I'm convinced that there's just one place where there's not any laughter, and that's hell.

Jerry Clower

A happy heart is like good medicine.
Proverbs 17:22 NCV

Let laughter reign when it comes. It is oil for the engines that rise to challenges and work miracles.

Donald E. Demaray

MORE WORDS FROM GOD'S WORD

*Nehemiah said, "Go and enjoy choice food and sweet drinks, and send
some to those who have nothing prepared. This day is sacred to our Lord.
Do not grieve, for the joy of the LORD is your strength."*

Nehemiah 8:10 NIV

Clap your hands, all you nations; shout to God with cries of joy.

Psalm 47:1 NIV

*. . . as the occasion when Jews got relief from their enemies, the month in
which their sorrow turned to joy, mourning somersaulted into a holiday for
parties and fun and laughter, the sending and receiving of presents and of
giving gifts to the poor.*

Esther 9:22 MSG

MY PRIORITIES FOR LIFE

I understand the importance of looking for the
humor in most situations.

I will think about ways that I can use humor as
a way to improve my own life and the lives of
the people around me.

There is joy and humor in everyday life . . . I will
pay attention to the right things.

Check Your Priority		
High	Med.	Low
—	—	—
—	—	—
—	—	—

Mistakes: The Price of Being Human

Therefore, if anyone is in Christ, he is a new creation;
the old has gone, the new has come!

2 Corinthians 5:17 NIV

Every man makes mistakes, and so will you. In fact, Winston Churchill once observed, "Success is going from failure to failure without loss of enthusiasm." What was good for Churchill is also good for you. You should expect to make mistakes—plenty of mistakes—but you should not allow those missteps to rob you of the enthusiasm you need to fulfill God's plan for your life.

We are imperfect people living in an imperfect world; mistakes are simply part of the price we pay for being here. But, even though mistakes are an inevitable part of life's journey, repeated mistakes should not be. When we commit the inevitable blunders of life, we must correct them, learn from them, and pray for the wisdom not to repeat them. When we do, our mistakes become lessons, and our lives become adventures in growth, not stagnation.

When our shortcomings are made public, we may feel embarrassed or worse. We may presume (quite incorrectly) that "everybody" is concerned with the gravity of our problem.

And, as a consequence, we may feel the need to hide from our problems rather than confront them. To do so is wrong. Even when our pride is bruised, we must face up to our mistakes and seek to rise above them.

Have you made a king-sized blunder or two? Of course you have. But here's the big question: have you used your mistakes as stumbling blocks or stepping stones? The answer to this question will determine how well you perform in the workplace and in every other aspect of your life. So don't let the fear of past failures hold you back. And remember this: Even if you've make a colossal mistake, God isn't finished with you yet—in fact, He's probably just getting started.

Lord, when we are wrong, make us willing to change;
and when we are right, make us easy to live with.

Peter Marshall

PRIORITIES FOR MY LIFE

Fix it sooner rather than later: When you make a mistake, the time to make things better is now, not later! The sooner you address your problem, the better.

TIMELESS WISDOM FOR GODLY LIVING

God's faithfulness has never depended on the faithfulness of his children.... God is greater than our weakness. In fact, I think, it is our weakness that reveals how great God is.

Max Lucado

There is nothing wrong with asking God's direction. But it is wrong to go our own way, then expect Him to bail us out.

Larry Burkett

Very few things motivate us to give God our undivided attention like being faced with the negative consequences of our decisions.

Charles Stanley

I hope you don't mind me telling you all this. One can learn only by seeing one's mistakes.

C. S. Lewis

If we confess our sins to him, he is faithful and just to forgive us and to cleanse us from every wrong.
1 John 1:9 NLT

Mature people are not emotionally and spiritually devastated by every mistake they make. They are able to maintain some kind of balance in their lives.

Joyce Meyer

MORE WORDS FROM GOD'S WORD

Have mercy on me, O God, according to your unfailing love; according to your great compassion blot out my transgressions. Wash away all my iniquity and cleanse me from my sin.

Psalm 51:1-2 NIV

You were taught, with regard to your former way of life, to put off your old self, which is being corrupted by its deceitful desires; to be made new in the attitude of your minds; and to put on the new self, created to be like God in true righteousness and holiness.

Ephesians 4:22-24 NIV

Therefore if any man be in Christ, he is a new creature: old things are passed away; behold, all things are become new.

2 Corinthians 5:17 KJV

MY PRIORITIES FOR LIFE

I believe that it is important to examine my mistakes in order to improve my work.

I understand that a mistake is never permanent (unless I do nothing to fix it).

When I make a mistake, I will learn something . . . and then I will forgive myself.

Check Your Priority		
High	Med.	Low
—	—	—
—	—	—
—	—	—

Accepting His Peace

I leave you peace; my peace I give you.
I do not give it to you as the world does.
So don't let your hearts be troubled or afraid.

John 14:27 NCV

As a busy man, your plate is probably full: work to do, bills to pay, a family to lead. Sometimes, it seems that you can scarcely find a moment's peace. But the beautiful words of John 14:27 are a reminder that God's peace is always available to you.

Jesus said, "Peace I leave with you, my peace I give unto you...." Christ offers us peace, not as the world gives, but as He alone gives. We, as believers, can accept His peace or ignore it.

When we accept the peace of Jesus Christ into our hearts, our lives are transformed. And then, because we possess the gift of peace, we can share that gift with fellow Christians, family members, friends, and associates. If, on the other hand, we choose to ignore the gift of peace—for whatever reason—we simply cannot share what we do not possess.

Today, as a gift to yourself, to your family, and to your friends, claim the inner peace that is your spiritual birthright: the peace of Jesus Christ. It is offered freely; it has been paid for in full; it is yours for the asking. So ask. And then share.

Put God underneath all your life,
and your life must rest upon the everlasting arms.

Phillips Brooks

And the peace of God, which surpasses all understanding,
will guard your hearts and minds through Christ Jesus.
Finally, brethren, whatever things are true, whatever things are noble,
whatever things are just, whatever things are pure, whatever things
are lovely, whatever things are of good report, if there is any virtue
and if there is anything praiseworthy—meditate on these things.

Philippians 4:7-8 NKJV

PRIORITIES FOR MY LIFE

Sometimes peace is a scarce commodity in a demanding, 21st century world. How can we find the peace that we so desperately desire? By turning our days and our lives over to God. May we give our lives, our hopes, and our prayers to the Father, and, by doing so, accept His will and His peace.

TIMELESS WISDOM FOR GODLY LIVING

A peaceful man does more good than a learned one.

Pope John XXIII

A peaceful heart finds joy in all of life's simple pleasures.

Anonymous

Where the Spirit of the Lord is, there is peace; where the Spirit of the Lord is, there is love.

Stephen R. Adams

Great peace is with the meek man, but in the heart of the proud man is always envy and indignation.

Thomas à Kempis

If your sinful nature controls your mind,
there is death. But if the Holy Spirit controls your mind,
there is life and peace.
Romans 8:6 NLT

When we learn to say a deep, passionate yes to the things that really matter, then peace begins to settle onto our lives like golden sunlight sifting to a forest floor.

Thomas Kinkade

MORE WORDS FROM GOD'S WORD

If it is possible, as far as it depends on you, live at peace with everyone.

Romans 12:18 NIV

Blessed are the peacemakers, for they will be called sons of God.

Matthew 5:9 NIV

God has called us to peace.

1 Corinthians 7:15 NKJV

Live peaceful and quiet lives in all godliness and holiness.

1 Timothy 2:2 NIV

MY PRIORITIES FOR LIFE

The value that I place on living a peaceful life . . .

Experience teaches me that peace is found by living in the center of God's will.

I find that the more time I spend in prayer, the more peaceful I feel.

Check Your Priority		
High	Med.	Low
—	—	—
—	—	—
—	—	—

The Power of Prayer

"'Relax, Daniel,' he continued, 'don't be afraid.
From the moment you decided to humble yourself to receive
understanding, your prayer was heard, and I set out to come to you.'"

Daniel 10:12 MSG

Is prayer an integral part of your daily life or is it a hit-or-miss habit? Do you "pray without ceasing," or is your prayer life an afterthought? Do you regularly pray in the quiet moments of the early morning, or do you bow your head only when others are watching?

As Christians, we are instructed to pray often. But it is important to note that genuine prayer requires much more than bending our knees and closing our eyes. Heartfelt prayer is an attitude of the heart.

If your prayers have become more a matter of habit than a matter of passion, you're robbing yourself of a deeper relationship with God. And how can you rectify this situation? By praying more frequently and more fervently. When you do, God will shower you with His blessings, His grace, and His love.

The quality of your spiritual life will be in direct proportion to the quality of your prayer life: the more you pray, the closer you will feel to God. So today, instead of turning things over in your mind, turn them over to God in prayer. Instead of worrying about your next decision, ask God to lead the way. Don't limit your prayers to the dinner table or the bedside table. Pray constantly about things great and small. God is always listening; it's up to you to do the rest.

When I pray, coincidences happen,
and when I don't, they don't.

William Temple

The best and sweetest flowers of Paradise
God gives to his people when they are upon their knees.
Prayer is the gate of heaven, a key to let us into Paradise.

Thomas Brooks

PRIORITIES FOR MY LIFE

Pray early and often: One way to make sure that your heart is in tune with God is to pray often. The more you talk to God, the more He will talk to you.

TIMELESS WISDOM FOR GODLY LIVING

There is nothing that makes us love a man so much as praying for him.

William Law

Why do so many Christians pray such tiny prayers when their God is so big?

Watchman Nee

My dad was a minister. My wife's father is a priest at an Episcopal church. All these years, I knew prayer worked. But to see it work on me and to experience it was a whole new revelation.

Tony Brown

Ask and it shall be given to you; seek and you shall find; knock and it shall be opened to you.
For every one who asks receives, and he who seeks finds, and to him who knocks it shall be opened.
Matthew 7:7-8 NASB

The things, good Lord, that I pray for, give me the grace to labor for.

St. Thomas More

MORE WORDS FROM GOD'S WORD

Rejoice always, pray without ceasing, in everything give thanks; for this is the will of God in Christ Jesus for you.

1 Thessalonians 5:16-18 NKJV

I want men everywhere to lift up holy hands in prayer, without anger or disputing.

1 Timothy 2:8 NIV

If my people who are called by my name, will humble themselves and pray and seek my face and turn from their wicked ways, then will I hear from heaven and will forgive their sin and will heal their land.

2 Chronicles 7:14 NIV

I sought the LORD, and he heard me, and delivered me from all my fears.

Psalm 34:4 KJV

MY PRIORITIES FOR LIFE

| | Check Your Priority | |
High	Med.	Low

I understand that prayer strengthens my relationship with God.

— — —

I trust that God will care for me, even when it seems that my prayers have gone unanswered.

— — —

I believe that my prayers have the power to change my circumstances, my perspective, and my future.

— — —

Real Repentance

*I preached that they should repent and turn to God
and prove their repentance by their deeds.*

Acts 26:20 NIV

Who among us has sinned? All of us. But, God calls upon us to turn away from sin by following His commandments. And the good news is this: When we do ask for God's forgiveness and turn our hearts to Him, He forgives us absolutely and completely.

We cannot sin against God without consequence. We cannot live outside His will without injury. We cannot distance ourselves from God without hardening our hearts. We cannot yield to the ever-tempting distractions of our world and, at the same time, enjoy God's peace.

Sometimes, in a futile attempt to justify our behaviors, we make a distinction between "big" sins and "little" ones. To do so is a mistake of "big" proportions. Sins of all shapes and sizes have the power to do us great harm. And in a world where sin is big business, that's certainly a sobering thought.

Genuine repentance requires more than simply offering God apologies for our misdeeds. Real repentance may start with feelings of sorrow and remorse, but it ends only when we turn away from the sin that has heretofore distanced us from our Creator. In truth, we offer our most meaningful apologies to

God, not with our words, but with our actions. As long as we are still engaged in sin, we may be "repenting," but we have not fully "repented."

God's Word teaches that when we invite Christ to rule over our lives, we become new beings: "You were taught to leave your old self—to stop living the evil way you lived before. That old self becomes worse, because people are fooled by the evil things they want to do. But you were taught to be made new in your hearts, to become a new person. That new person is made to be like God—made to be truly good and holy." (Ephesians 4:22-24 NCV)

Is there an aspect of your life that is preventing you from becoming a new person in Christ? Are you engaged in an activity that is distancing you from your God? If so, ask for His forgiveness, and—just as importantly—stop sinning. Then, wrap yourself in the protection of God's Word. When you do, you will be secure.

Repentance becomes a way of life, a lifelong process of turning towards the Holy One, that happens one day at a time.

Trevor Hudson

PRIORITIES FOR MY LIFE

First, confess your sins to God. Then, ask Him what actions you should take in order to make things right again.

TIMELESS WISDOM FOR GODLY LIVING

Radical repentance is indispensable for conversion. Unless we recognize our failure and need, we will not cry out to God to save us.

Stanley Grenz

Repentance is the returning from the unnatural to the natural state, from the Devil to God, through discipline and effort.

St. John of Damascus

Repentance is the first conscious movement of the soul away from sin and toward God.

Sam Jones

The bedrock of Christianity is repentance.

Oswald Chambers

> *Come back to the LORD and live!*
> Amos 5:6 NLT

Repentance is the golden key that opens the palace of eternity.

John Milton

MORE WORDS FROM GOD'S WORD

You were taught to leave your old self—to stop living the evil way you lived before. That old self becomes worse, because people are fooled by the evil things they want to do. But you were taught to be made new in your hearts, to become a new person. That new person is made to be like God—made to be truly good and holy.

Ephesians 4:22–24 NCV

There will be more joy in heaven over one sinner who repents than over 99 righteous people who don't need repentance.

Luke 15:7 Holman CSB

All the prophets testify about Him that through His name everyone who believes in Him will receive forgiveness of sins.

Acts 10:43 Holman CSB

MY PRIORITIES FOR LIFE

| | Check Your Priority | |
High	Med.	Low

I understand that sin is destructive.

— — —

I understand that the consequences of my actions may be hurtful to my loved ones as well as myself.

— — —

I believe true repentance requires action that turns me away from my sins.

— — —

Sharing
the Good News

Now then we are ambassadors for Christ . . . .

2 Corinthians 5:20 KJV

Are you a bashful Christian, one who is afraid to speak up for your Savior? Do you allow others to share their testimonies while you stand on the sidelines, reluctant to share yours? After His resurrection, Jesus addressed His disciples: "But the eleven disciples proceeded to Galilee, to the mountain which Jesus had designated. When they saw Him, they worshiped Him; but some were doubtful. And Jesus came up and spoke to them, saying, "All authority has been given to Me in heaven and on earth. "Go therefore and make disciples of all the nations, baptizing them in the name of the Father and the Son and the Holy Spirit, teaching them to observe all that I commanded you; and lo, I am with you always, even to the end of the age." (Matthew 28:16-20 NASB)

Christ's great commission applies to Christians of every generation, including our own. As believers, we are called to share the Good News of Jesus Christ with our families, with our neighbors, and with the world. Yet many of us are slow to obey the last commandment of the risen Christ; we simply don't do our best to "make disciples of all the nations." Although our personal testimonies are vitally important, we sometimes hesitate to share our experiences. And that's unfortunate.

Billy Graham observed, "Our faith grows by expression. If we want to keep our faith, we must share it." If you are a follower of Christ, the time to express your belief in Him is now.

You know how Jesus has touched your heart; help Him do the same for others. You must do likewise, and you must do so today. Tomorrow may indeed be too late.

Send the light, the blessed gospel light;
let it shine from shore to shore!

Charles H. Gabriel

The wise Christian will watch for opportunities to do good,
to speak the life-bringing word to sinners,
to pray the rescuing prayer of intercession.

A. W. Tozer

PRIORITIES FOR MY LIFE

Don't be embarrassed to discuss your faith: You need not have attended seminary to have worthwhile opinions about your faith. Express those opinions, especially to your children; your kids need to know where you stand.

TIMELESS WISDOM FOR GODLY LIVING

The glory of God, and, as our only means of glorifying Him, the salvation of human souls, is the real business of life.

C. S. Lewis

The evangelistic harvest is always urgent. The destiny of men and of nations is always being decided. Every generation is strategic. We are not responsible for the past generation, and we cannot bear the full responsibility for the next one, but we do have our generation. God will hold us responsible as to how well we fulfill our responsibilities to this age and take advantage of our opportunities.

Billy Graham

I will also make You a light of the nations so that My salvation may reach to the end of the earth.
Isaiah 49:6 NASB

If you are a Christian, then you are a minister. A non-ministering Christian is a contradiction in terms.

Elton Trueblood

MORE WORDS FROM GOD'S WORD

After this the Lord appointed 70 others, and He sent them ahead of Him in pairs to every town and place where He Himself was about to go. He told them: "The harvest is abundant, but the workers are few. Therefore, pray to the Lord of the harvest to send out workers into His harvest. Now go; I'm sending you out like lambs among wolves."

Luke 10:1-3 Holman CSB

Then He said to them, "Go into all the world and preach the gospel to the whole creation."

Mark 16:15 Holman CSB

This good news of the kingdom will be proclaimed in all the world as a testimony to all nations.

Matthew 24:14 Holman CSB

MY PRIORITIES FOR LIFE

For me, the importance of sharing the Gospel message is . . .

I believe that God will empower me to share my faith.

I try to be sensitive for unplanned opportunities to share the Good News of Jesus Christ.

Check Your Priority		
High	Med.	Low
—	—	—
—	—	—
—	—	—

Making the Most of Our Talents

God has given gifts to each of you from his great variety of spiritual gifts.
Manage them well so that God's generosity can flow through you.

1 Peter 4:10 NLT

All of us have special talents, and you are no exception. But your talent is no guarantee of success; it must be cultivated and nurtured; otherwise, it will go unused . . . and God's gift to you will be squandered.

God knew precisely what He was doing when He gave you a unique set of talents and opportunities. And now, God wants you to use those talents for the glory of His kingdom. But you live in a world that often encourages you to do otherwise.

You inhabit a world that is filled to the brim with countless opportunities to squander your time, your resources, and your talents. So you must be watchful for distractions and temptations that might lead you astray.

Your particular talent is a treasure on temporary loan from God. He intends that your talent enrich the world and enrich your life. If you're sincerely interested in building a better life, build it upon the talents that God (in His infinite wisdom) has given you. Don't try to build a career (or a life) around the talents you wish He had given you.

God has blessed you with unique opportunities to serve Him, and He has given you every tool that you need to do so. Today, accept this challenge: value the talent that God has given you, nourish it, make it grow, and share it with the world. After all, the best way to say "Thank You" for God's gifts is to use them.

Employ whatever God has entrusted you with,
in doing good, all possible good,
in every possible kind and degree.

John Wesley

PRIORITIES FOR MY LIFE

Converting talent into skill requires work: Each of us possesses special abilities that can be nurtured carefully or ignored totally. Our challenge, of course, is to do the former and to avoid the latter.

TIMELESS WISDOM FOR GODLY LIVING

If you want to reach your potential, you need to add a strong work ethic to your talent.

John Maxwell

God often reveals His direction for our lives through the way He made us...with a certain personality and unique skills.

Bill Hybels

What we are is God's gift to us. What we become is our gift to God.

Anonymous

You are the only person on earth who can use your ability.

Zig Ziglar

Do not neglect the gift that is in you.
1 Timothy 4:14 Holman CSB

Discipline is the refining fire by which talent becomes ability.

Roy L. Smith

MORE WORDS FROM GOD'S WORD

There are different kinds of gifts, but they are all from the same Spirit. There are different ways to serve but the same Lord to serve.

1 Corinthians 12:4–5 NCV

The man who had received the five talents brought the other five. "Master," he said, "you entrusted me with five talents. See, I have gained five more." His master replied, "Well done, good and faithful servant! You have been faithful with a few things; I will put you in charge of many things. Come and share your master's happiness."

Matthew 25:20-21 NIV

Every good gift and every perfect gift is from above, and cometh down from the Father of lights.

James 1:17 KJV

MY PRIORITIES FOR LIFE

I believe that God wants me to take risks to do the work that He intends for me to do.

I believe that it is important to associate with people who encourage me to use my talents.

I believe that it is important to honor God by using the talents He has given me.

Check Your Priority		
High	Med.	Low
—	—	—
—	—	—
—	—	—

The Right Kind of Wisdom

The Lord says, "I will make you wise and show you where to go.
I will guide you and watch over you."

Psalm 32:8 NCV

Do you place a high value on the acquisition of wisdom? If so, you are not alone; most people would like to be wise, but not everyone is willing to do the work that is required to become wise. Wisdom is not like a mushroom; it does not spring up overnight. It is, instead, like an oak tree that starts as a tiny acorn, grows into a sapling, and eventually reaches up to the sky, tall and strong.

To become wise, you must seek God's guidance and live according to His Word. To become wise, you must seek instruction with consistency and purpose. To become wise, you must not only learn the lessons of the Christian life, but you must also live by them. But oftentimes, that's easier said than done.

Sometimes, amid the demands of daily life, you will lose perspective. Life may seem out of balance, and the pressures of everyday living may seem overwhelming. What's needed is a fresh perspective, a restored sense of balance . . . and God's wisdom. If you call upon the Lord and seek to see the world through

His eyes, He will give you guidance, wisdom and perspective. When you make God's priorities your priorities, He will lead you according to His plan and according to His commandments. When you study God's teachings, you are reminded that God's reality is the ultimate reality.

Do you seek to live a life of righteousness and wisdom? If so, you must study the ultimate source of wisdom: the Word of God. You must seek out worthy mentors and listen carefully to their advice. You must associate, day in and day out, with godly men and women. Then, as you accumulate wisdom, you must not keep it for yourself; you must, instead, share it with your friends and family members.

But be forewarned: if you sincerely seek to share your hard-earned wisdom with others, your actions must reflect the values that you hold dear. The best way to share your wisdom—perhaps the only way—is not by your words, but by your example.

PRIORITIES FOR MY LIFE

Wisdom 101: If you're looking for wisdom, the Book of Proverbs is a wonderful place to start. It has 31 chapters, one for each day of the month. If you read Proverbs regularly, and if you take its teachings to heart, you'll gain timeless wisdom from God's unchanging Word.

TIMELESS WISDOM FOR GODLY LIVING

The person who is wise spiritually, who is a true Christian, builds his life and performs his duties carefully, realizing the great substance and importance involved.

John MacArthur

The fruit of wisdom is Christlikeness, peace, humility, and love. And, the root of it is faith in Christ as the manifested wisdom of God.

J. I. Packer

Wisdom is the God-given ability to see life with rare objectivity and to handle life with rare stability.

Charles Swindoll

The essence of wisdom, from a practical standpoint, is pausing long enough to look at our lives—invitations, opportunities, relationships—from God's perspective. And then acting on it.

Charles Stanley

Wisdom is the principal thing; therefore get wisdom. And in all your getting, get understanding.
Proverbs 4:7 NKJV

God's plan for our guidance is for us to grow gradually in wisdom before we get to the crossroads.

Bill Hybels

MORE WORDS FROM GOD'S WORD

Happy is the person who finds wisdom, the one who gets understanding.

Proverbs 3:13 NCV

But the wisdom that is from above is first pure, then peaceable, gentle, willing to yield, full of mercy and good fruits, without partiality and without hypocrisy.

James 3:17 NKJV

Let the word of Christ dwell in you richly in all wisdom; teaching and admonishing one another in psalms and hymns and spiritual songs, singing with grace in your hearts to the Lord.

Colossians 3:16 KJV

MY PRIORITIES FOR LIFE

	Check Your Priority	
	High Med. Low	

I will continually remind myself of God's wisdom by reading the Bible each day.

— — —

I will do my best to live wisely by obeying the teachings that I find in God's Word.

— — —

I will associate with wise men and wise women.

— — —

I will share my wisdom with friends and family members who seek my advice.

— — —

Cheerful Christianity

Be cheerful. Keep things in good repair. Keep your spirits up.
Think in harmony. Be agreeable. Do all that,
and the God of love and peace will be with you for sure.

2 Corinthians 13:11 MSG

Cheerfulness is a gift that we give to others and to ourselves. And, as believers who have been saved by a risen Christ, why shouldn't we be cheerful? The answer, of course, is that we have every reason to honor our Savior with joy in our hearts, smiles on our faces, and words of celebration on our lips.

Few things in life are more sad, or, for that matter, more absurd, than the sight of grumpy Christians trudging unhappily through life. Christ promises us lives of abundance and joy if we accept His love and His grace. Yet sometimes, even the most righteous among us are beset by fits of ill temper and frustration. During these moments, we may not feel like turning our thoughts and prayers to Christ, but that's precisely what we should do.

Mrs. Charles E. Cowman, the author of the classic devotional text, *Streams in the Desert*, wrote, "Two wings are necessary to lift our souls toward God: prayer and praise. Prayer asks. Praise accepts the answer." That's why we should find the time to lift our concerns to God in prayer, and to praise Him for all that He has done.

John Wesley correctly observed, "Sour godliness is the devil's religion." These words remind us that pessimism and doubt are some of the most important tools that Satan uses to achieve his objectives. Our challenge, of course, is to ensure that Satan cannot use these tools on us.

Are you a cheerful Christian? You should be! And what is the best way to attain the joy that is rightfully yours? By giving Christ what is rightfully His: your heart, your soul, and your life.

Be merry, really merry. The life of a true Christian should be a perpetual jubilee, a prelude to the festivals of eternity.

Theophare Venard

PRIORITIES FOR MY LIFE

Do you need a little cheering up? If so, find somebody else who needs cheering up, too. Then, do your best to brighten that person's day. When you do, you'll discover that cheering up other people is a wonderful way to cheer yourself up, too!

TIMELESS WISDOM FOR GODLY LIVING

It is not fitting, when one is in God's service, to have a gloomy face or a chilling look.

St. Francis of Assisi

Cheerfulness is no sin, nor is there any grace in a solemn cast of countenance.

John Newton

Hope is the power of being cheerful in circumstances which we know to be desperate.

G. K. Chesterton

When I think of God, my heart is so full of joy that the notes leap and dance as they leave my pen; and since God has given me a cheerful heart, I serve him with a cheerful spirit.

Franz Joseph Haydn

God loves a cheerful giver.
2 Corinthians 9:7 NIV

The people whom I have seen succeed best in life have always been cheerful and hopeful people who went about their business with a smile on their faces.

Charles Kingsley

MORE WORDS FROM GOD'S WORD

Jacob said, "For what a relief it is to see your friendly smile. It is like seeing the smile of God!"

Genesis 33:10 NLT

Do everything readily and cheerfully—no bickering, no second-guessing allowed! Go out into the world uncorrupted, a breath of fresh air in this squalid and polluted society. Provide people with a glimpse of good living and of the living God. Carry the light-giving Message into the night.

Philippians 2:14-15 MSG

A happy heart is like a continual feast.

Proverbs 15:15 NCV

MY PRIORITIES FOR LIFE

I will cheerfully acknowledge the many blessings that God has given me.

I will consider this day—and every day—to be a gift from God and a cause for celebration.

I will do my best to maintain a positive attitude and a cheerful disposition, even when I'm tired, or frustrated, or both.

I will focus my thoughts on opportunities, not problems.

Check Your Priority		
High	Med.	Low
—	—	—
—	—	—
—	—	—
—	—	—

Spiritual Maturity, Day by Day

*Don't become so well-adjusted to your culture that you fit into it
without even thinking. Instead, fix your attention on God.
You'll be changed from the inside out. Readily recognize what he wants
from you, and quickly respond to it. Unlike the culture around you,
always dragging you down to its level of immaturity, God brings
the best out of you, develops well-formed maturity in you.*

Romans 12:2 MSG

God doesn't intend for you to be a stagnant believer. Far from it! God's plan for you includes a lifetime of prayer, praise, and spiritual growth.

As Christians, we can and should continue to grow in the love and the knowledge of our Savior as long as we live. When we cease to grow, either emotionally or spiritually, we do ourselves and our loved ones a profound disservice. But, if we study God's Word, if we obey His commandments, and if we live in the protection of His will, we will not be "stagnant" believers; we will, instead, be growing Christians . . . and that's exactly what God wants for our lives.

If we are to be the kind of righteous Christian men that God intends, we must continue to grow in our knowledge and love of the Lord. In those quiet moments when we open our hearts to God, the One who made us keeps remaking us. He gives us direction, perspective, wisdom, and courage.

Are you continually seeking to become a more mature believer? Hopefully so, because that's exactly what you owe to yourself and to God . . . but not necessarily in that order.

Being a Christian means accepting the terms of creation, accepting God as our maker and redeemer, and growing day by day into an increasingly glorious creature in Christ, developing joy, experiencing love, maturing in peace.

Eugene Peterson

PRIORITIES FOR MY LIFE

Spiritual maturity is a journey, not a destination. And the sooner you begin that journey, the farther you're likely to go.

TIMELESS WISDOM FOR GODLY LIVING

Being childlike is commendable. Being childish is unacceptable.

Charles Swindoll

The process of growing up is to me valued for what we gain, not for what we lose.

C. S. Lewis

When I was young I was sure of everything; in a few years, having been mistaken a thousand times, I was not half so sure of most things as I was before; at present, I am hardly sure of anything but what God has revealed to me.

John Wesley

Let the wise listen and add to their learning,
and let the discerning get guidance.
Proverbs 1:5 NIV

There are two things we are called to do: we are to depend on His strength and be obedient to His Word. If we can't handle being dependent and obedient, we will never become the kind of people who have a heart for God.

Stuart Briscoe

MORE WORDS FROM GOD'S WORD

Therefore let us leave the elementary teachings about Christ and go on to maturity . . . .

Hebrews 6:1 NIV

But endurance must do its complete work, so that you may be mature and complete, lacking nothing.

James 1:4 Holman CSB

There has never been the slightest doubt in my mind that the God who started this great work in you would keep at it and bring it to a flourishing finish on the very day Christ Jesus appears.

Philippians 1:6 MSG

MY PRIORITIES FOR LIFE

I believe that the level of my spiritual maturity has a direct impact, either positively or negatively, on those around me.

Since I believe that I still have "room to grow" in my faith, gaining spiritual maturity remains a priority for me.

Since I feel that spiritual growth happens day by day, and I will live, worship, and pray accordingly.

Check Your Priority		
High	Med.	Low
—	—	—
—	—	—
—	—	—

The Positive Path

Because the eyes of the Lord are on the righteous
and His ears are open to their request.
But the face of the Lord is against those who do evil.

1 Peter 3:12 Holman CSB

If you're like most men, you seek the admiration of your neighbors, your coworkers, and, most importantly, your family members. But the eagerness to please others should never overshadow your eagerness to please God. If you seek to fulfill the purposes that God has in store for you, then you must seek to please Him first and always.

Matthew 6:33 reminds us that when we allow God to reign in our hearts, He will provide for us. Each new day presents countless opportunities to put God in first place . . . or not. When we honor Him by living according to His commandments, we earn for ourselves the abundance and peace that He promises. But, when we concern ourselves more with pleasing others than with pleasing our Creator, we bring needless suffering upon ourselves and our families.

Would you like a time-tested formula for successful living? Here is a formula that is proven and true: Seek God's approval in every aspect of your life. Does this sound too simple? Perhaps it is simple, but it is also the only way to reap the marvelous riches that God has in store for You.

It may be said without qualification that every man
is as holy and as full of the Spirit as he wants to be.
He may not be as full as he wishes he were,
but he is most certainly as full as he wants to be.

A. W. Tozer

And now, Israel, what does the Lord your God ask of you
except to fear the Lord your God by walking in all His ways,
to love Him, and to worship the Lord your God
with all your heart and all your soul?

Deuteronomy 10:12 Holman CSB

PRIORITIES FOR MY LIFE

Righteous living leads to joy. Bill Hybels observes, "Christianity
says we were created by a righteous God to flourish and be
exhilarated in a righteous environment. God has "wired" us
in such a way that the more righteous we are, the more we'll
actually enjoy life." Holy living doesn't take the joy out of life, it
puts it in.

TIMELESS WISDOM FOR GODLY LIVING

A life growing in its purity and devotion will be a more prayerful life.

E. M. Bounds

If we don't hunger and thirst after righteousness, we'll become anemic and feel miserable in our Christian experience.

Franklin Graham

We must appropriate the tender mercy of God every day after conversion, or problems quickly develop. We need his grace daily in order to live a righteous life.

Jim Cymbala

Our progress in holiness depends on God and ourselves—on God's grace and on our will to be holy.

Mother Teresa

Therefore, come out from among them and be separate, says the Lord; do not touch any unclean thing, and I will welcome you.

2 Corinthians 6:17 Holman CSB

A man who lives right, and is right, has more power in his silence than another has by his words.

Phillips Brooks

MORE WORDS FROM GOD'S WORD

Flee from youthful passions, and pursue righteousness, faith, love, and peace, along with those who call on the Lord from a pure heart.

2 Timothy 2:22 Holman CSB

Do what is right and good in the Lord's sight, so that you may prosper and so that you may enter and possess the good land the Lord your God swore to [give] your fathers.

Deuteronomy 6:18 Holman CSB

Sow righteousness for yourselves and reap faithful love; break up your untilled ground. It is time to seek the Lord until He comes and sends righteousness on you like the rain.

Hosea 10:12 Holman CSB

MY PRIORITIES FOR LIFE

I study God's Word each day, and I strive to understand God's teachings.

I seek to live in accordance with Biblical teachings.

I surround myself with like-minded believers who seek to obey God's Word.

I assiduously avoid people and places that might tempt me to disobey God's commandments.

Check Your Priority		
High	Med.	Low
—	—	—
—	—	—
—	—	—
—	—	—

Renewal Day by Day

The One who was sitting on the throne said,
"Look! I am making everything new!" Then he said,
"Write this, because these words are true and can be trusted."

Revelation 21:5 NCV

When we genuinely lift our hearts and prayers to God, He renews our strength. Are you almost too weary to lift your head? Then bow it. Offer your concerns and your fears to your Father in Heaven. He is always at your side, offering His love and His strength.

Sometimes, the demands of daily life can drain us of our strength and rob us of the joy that is rightfully ours in Christ. When we find ourselves tired, discouraged, or worse, there is a source from which we can draw the power needed to recharge our spiritual batteries. That source is God.

God intends that His children lead joyous lives filled with abundance and peace. But sometimes, abundance and peace seem very far away. It is then that we must turn to God for renewal, and when we do, He will restore us.

Are you troubled or anxious? Take your anxieties to God in prayer. Are you weak or worried? Delve deeply into God's Holy Word and sense His presence in the quiet moments of the early morning. Are you spiritually exhausted? Call upon fellow believers to support you, and call upon Christ to renew your spirit and your life. Your Savior will never let you down. To the contrary, He will always lift you up if you ask Him to. So what, dear friend, are you waiting for?

Christ came when all things were growing old.
He made them new.

St. Augustine

Come to Me, all you who labor and are heavy laden,
and I will give you rest. Take My yoke upon you and learn from Me,
for I am gentle and lowly in heart, and you will find rest for your souls.
For My yoke is easy and My burden is light.

Matthew 11:28-30 NKJV

PRIORITIES FOR MY LIFE

God is in the business of making all things new: Vance Havner correctly observed, "God is not running an antique shop! He is making all things new!" And that includes you.

TIMELESS WISDOM FOR GODLY LIVING

Resolutely slam and lock the door on past sin and failure, and throw away the key.

Oswald Chambers

Walking with God leads to receiving his intimate counsel, and counseling leads to deep restoration.

John Eldredge

The well of God's forgiveness never runs dry.

Grady Nutt

Do not lose faith in God. The grace He gives will be in direct proportion to the amount of sufferings you must bear. No one else can do this except the Creator who made us and knows how to renew our strength by His grace.

Fénelon

*When doubts filled my mind,
your comfort gave me renewed hope and cheer.*
Psalm 94:19 NLT

One reason so much American Christianity is a mile wide and an inch deep is that Christians are simply tired. Sometimes you need to kick back and rest for Jesus' sake.

Dennis Swanberg

MORE WORDS FROM GOD'S WORD

Create in me a pure heart, O God, and renew a steadfast spirit within me. Do not cast me from your presence or take your Holy Spirit from me. Restore to me the joy of your salvation and grant me a willing spirit, to sustain me.

Psalm 51:10-12 NIV

He makes me to lie down in green pastures; He leads me beside the still waters. He restores my soul; He leads me in the paths of righteousness For His name's sake.

Psalm 23:2–3 NKJV

You are being renewed in the spirit of your minds; you put on the new man, the one created according to God's likeness in righteousness and purity of the truth.

Ephesians 4:23-24 Holman CSB

MY PRIORITIES FOR LIFE

I believe that God can make all things new . . . including me.

I take time each day to be still and let God give me perspective and direction.

I understand the importance of getting adequate sleep and sensible exercise.

Check Your Priority		
High	Med.	Low
—	—	—
—	—	—
—	—	—

Finding Contentment in a Discontented World

But godliness with contentment is great gain. For we brought nothing into the world, and we can take nothing out of it.
But if we have food and clothing, we will be content with that.

1 Timothy 6:6-8 NIV

When we conduct ourselves in ways that are opposed to God's commandments, we rob ourselves of God's peace. When we fall prey to the temptations and distractions of our irreverent age, we rob ourselves of God's blessings. When we become preoccupied with material possessions or personal status, we forfeit the contentment that is rightfully ours in Christ.

Where can we find lasting contentment? Is it a result of wealth, or power, or fame? Hardly. Genuine contentment is a gift from God to those who follow His commandments and accept His Son. When Christ dwells at the center of our families and our lives, contentment will belong to us just as surely as we belong to Him. Do you seek happiness, abundance, and contentment? If so, here are some things you should do: Love God and His Son; depend upon God for strength; try, to the best of your abilities, to follow God's will; and strive to obey His Holy Word. When you do these things, you'll discover that happiness goes hand-in-hand with righteousness. The happiest people are not those who rebel against God; the happiest people are those who love God and obey His commandments.

What does life have in store for you? A world full of possibilities (of course it's up to you to seize them), and God's promise of abundance (of course it's up to you to accept it). So, as you embark upon the next phase of your journey, remember to celebrate the life that God has given you. Your Creator has blessed you beyond measure. Honor Him with your prayers, your words, your deeds, and your joy.

Are you a thoroughly contented Christian? If so, then you are well aware of the healing power of the risen Christ. But if your spirit is temporarily troubled, perhaps you need to focus less upon your own priorities and more upon God's priorities. When you do, you'll rediscover this life-changing truth: Genuine contentment begins with God . . . and ends there.

True contentment is the power of getting out of
any situation all that is in it.

G. K. Chesterton

PRIORITIES FOR MY LIFE

Be contented where you are . . . even if it's not exactly where you want to end up. God has something wonderful in store for you—and remember that God's timing is perfect—so be patient, trust God, do your best, and expect the best.

TIMELESS WISDOM FOR GODLY LIVING

God is most glorified in us when we are most satisfied in him.

John Piper

Next to faith this is the highest art: to be content with the calling in which God has placed you. I have not learned it yet.

Martin Luther

Contentment is difficult because nothing on earth can satisfy our deepest longing. We long to see God.

Max Lucado

The life of strain is difficult. The life of inner peace—a life that comes from a positive attitude—is the easiest type of existence.

Norman Vincent Peale

Let your character be free from the love of money, being content with what you have; for He Himself has said, "I will never desert you, nor will I ever forsake you."
Hebrews 13:5 NASB

Contentment is not escape from battle, but rather an abiding peace and confidence in the midst of battle.

Warren Wiersbe

MORE WORDS FROM GOD'S WORD

I've learned by now to be quite content whatever my circumstances. I'm just as happy with little as with much, with much as with little. I've found the recipe for being happy whether full or hungry, hands full or hands empty.

Philippians 4:11-12 MSG

A tranquil heart is life to the body, but jealousy is rottenness to the bones.

Proverbs 14:30 Holman CSB

Because your love is better than life, my lips will glorify you. I will praise you as long as I live, and in your name I will lift up my hands. My soul will be satisfied as with the richest of foods; with singing lips my mouth will praise you.

Psalm 63:3-5 NIV

MY PRIORITIES FOR LIFE

For me, the importance that I place on being contented is . . .

I understand that contentment comes, not from my circumstances, but from my attitude.

I believe that peace with God is the starting point for a contented life.

Check Your Priority		
High	Med.	Low
—	—	—
—	—	—
—	—	—

The Optimistic Christian

But if we look forward to something we don't have yet,
we must wait patiently and confidently.

Romans 8:25 NLT

Are you a hope-filled, enthusiastic Christian? You should be. After all, as a believer, you have every reason to be optimistic about your life here on earth and your eternal life in heaven. As English clergyman William Ralph Inge observed, "No Christian should be a pessimist, for Christianity is a system of radical optimism." Inge's words are most certainly true, but sometimes, you may find yourself pulled down by the inevitable concerns of everyday life. If you find yourself discouraged, exhausted, or both, then it's time to ask yourself this question: what's bothering you, and why?

If you're overly worried by the inevitable ups and downs of life, God wants to have a little chat with you. After all, God has made promises to you that He intends to keep. And if your life has been transformed by God's only begotten Son, then you, as a recipient of God's grace, have every reason to live courageously.

Are you willing to trust God's plans for your life? Hopefully, you will trust Him completely. After all, the words of the Psalmist make it clear: "The ways of God are without fault. The Lord's words are pure. He is a shield to those who trust him" (Psalm 18:30 NCV).

Woodroll Kroll noted, "If our minds are stayed upon God, His peace will rule the affairs entertained by our minds. If, on the other hand, we allow our minds to dwell on the cares of this world, God's peace will be far from our thoughts." These words should serve as a reminder that even when the challenges of the day seem daunting, God remains steadfast. And, so should you.

So make this promise to yourself and keep it—vow to be an expectant, faith-filled Christian. Think optimistically about your life, your profession, your family, your future, and your purpose for living. Trust your hopes, not your fears. Take time to celebrate God's glorious creation. And then, when you've filled your heart with hope and gladness, share your optimism with others. They'll be better for it, and so will you.

The people whom I have seen succeed best in life have always been cheerful and hopeful people who went about their business with a smile on their faces.

Charles Kingsley

PRIORITIES FOR MY LIFE

Be a realistic optimist: You should strive to think realistically about the future, but you should never confuse realism with pessimism. Your attitude toward the future will help create your future, so you might as well put the self-fulfilling prophecy to work for you by being both a realist and an optimist. And remember that life is far too short to be a pessimist.

TIMELESS WISDOM FOR GODLY LIVING

The essence of optimism is that it takes no account of the present, but it is a source of inspiration, of vitality, and of hope. Where others have resigned, it enables a man to hold his head high, to claim the future for himself, and not abandon it to his enemy.

Dietrich Bonhoeffer

There is wisdom in the habit of looking at the bright side of life.

Father Flanagan

Other men see only a hopeless end, but the Christian rejoices in an endless hope.

Gilbert M. Beeken

The popular idea of faith is of a certain obstinate optimism: the hope, tenaciously held in the face of trouble, that the universe is fundamentally friendly and things may get better.

J. I. Packer

Make me hear joy and gladness.
Psalm 51:8 NKJV

Those who keep speaking about the sun while walking under a cloudy sky are messengers of hope, the true saints of our day.

Henri Nouwen

MORE WORDS FROM GOD'S WORD

My cup runs over. Surely goodness and mercy shall follow me all the days of my life; and I will dwell in the house of the Lord forever.

Psalm 23:5-6 NKJV

I can do everything through him that gives me strength.

Philippians 4:13 NIV

The Lord is my light and my salvation; whom shall I fear? The Lord is the strength of my life; of whom shall I be afraid?

Psalm 27:1 KJV

MY PRIORITIES FOR LIFE

I understand the importance of counting my blessings, not my hardships.

I will look for opportunities, not obstructions; and I will look for possibilities, not problems.

I understand the need to associate with people who encourage me to be optimistic, upbeat, and cheerful.

I will share words of encouragement and hope with my family, with my friends, and with my coworkers.

Check Your Priority

High	Med.	Low
—	—	—
—	—	—
—	—	—
—	—	—

Christ-centered Leadership

Shepherd God's flock, for whom you are responsible.
Watch over them because you want to, not because you are forced.
That is how God wants it. Do it because you are happy to serve.

1 Peter 5:2 NCV

The old saying is familiar and true: imitation is the sincerest form of flattery. As believers, we are called to imitate, as best we can, the carpenter from Galilee. Imitating Christ is often difficult and sometimes impossible, but as Christians, we must continue to try.

This generation faces problems that defy easy solutions, yet face them we must. To do so, we need leaders whose vision is clear and whose intentions are pure. Daniel writes, "Those who are wise will shine like the brightness of the heavens, and those who lead many to righteousness, like the stars for ever and ever" (12:3 NIV). That's why our world needs leaders who willingly honor God with their words and their deeds, but not necessarily in that order.

If you seek to be such a leader, then you must begin by making yourself a worthy example to your family, to your friends, to your church, and to your community. After all, your words will always seem insincere unless you are willing to live by them.

Christ-centered leadership is always an exercise in service: service to God in heaven and service to His children here on earth. Christ willingly became a servant to His followers, and you must seek to do the same for yours. And as you serve others, you must also do your best to inspire them. How can you do so? By becoming genuinely inspired yourself.

Are you excited about serving God? And you are willing to encourage others to do likewise? Hopefully, you can answer those questions in the affirmative. Unfortunately, far too many Christians seem bored with their faith and stressed by their service. Don't allow yourself to become one of them! Serve God with thanksgiving in your heart and praise on your lips. Make your service to Him a time of celebration and praise. Worship your Creator by working for Him, joyfully, faithfully, and often.

And finally, ask yourself this question: Are you the kind of servant-leader whom you would want to follow? If so, congratulations: you are honoring your Savior by imitating Him. And that, of course, is the sincerest form of flattery.

PRIORITIES FOR MY LIFE

Think about your own leadership style. Remember that leadership comes in many forms and that you will probably be more effective using your own style, not by trying to copy someone else. When it comes to leadership, an original version of yourself is far better than a weak imitation of someone else.

TIMELESS WISDOM FOR GODLY LIVING

A wise leader chooses a variety of gifted individuals. He complements his strengths.

Charles Stanley

O Lord, build me a son whose heart will be clear, whose goal will be high, a son who will master himself before he seeks to master other men, one who will reach into the future, yet never forget the past.

General Douglas MacArthur

Greatness lies not in being strong, but in the right use of strength.

Henry Ward Beecher

The test of a leader is taking the vision from me to we.

John Maxwell

An overseer, then, must be above reproach, the husband of one wife, temperate, prudent, respectable, hospitable, able to teach, not addicted to wine or pugnacious, but gentle, peaceable, free from the love of money.

1 Timothy 3:2-3 NASB

The man who kneels before God will stand before men.

Leonard Ravenhill

MORE WORDS FROM GOD'S WORD

Those who are wise will shine like the brightness of the heavens, and those who lead many to righteousness, like the stars for ever and ever.

Daniel 12:3 NIV

But a good leader plans to do good, and those good things make him a good leader.

Isaiah 32:8 NCV

His lord said unto him, Well done, thou good and faithful servant: thou hast been faithful over a few things, I will make thee ruler over many things: enter thou into the joy of thy lord.

Matthew 25:21 KJV

MY PRIORITIES FOR LIFE

I believe that leadership comes in many forms, and that I can lead others in my own way using my own style.

I believe that leadership, like other abilities, should honor God.

I think it is important for me to develop my leadership skills.

Check Your Priority		
High	Med.	Low
—	—	—
—	—	—
—	—	—

The Disciplined Life

Do you not know that those who run in a race all run,
but only one receives the prize? Run in such a way that you may win.
Everyone who competes in the games exercises self-control in all things.

1 Corinthians 9:24-25 NASB

A re you a self-disciplined person? If so, congratulations . . . if not, it's time to think long and hard about your values, your priorities, and your habits.

God's Word makes it clear that He doesn't reward laziness, misbehavior, or apathy. To the contrary, He expects believers (like you) to behave with dignity and discipline.

You live in a world where leisure is glorified and indifference is often glamorized—but God has bigger things in store for you. He did not create you for a life of mediocrity; He created you for far greater things. God has given you a unique assortment of talents and opportunities . . . and He expects you to use them. But beware: it is not always easy to cultivate those talents.

Sometimes, you must invest countless hours (or, in some cases, many years) honing your skills. And that's perfectly okay with God, because He understands that self-discipline is a blessing, not a burden.

When you pause to consider how much work needs to be done, you'll realize that self-discipline is not simply a proven way to get ahead, it's also an integral part of God's plan for your life. If you genuinely seek to be faithful stewards of your time, your talents, and your resources, you must adopt a disciplined approach to life. Otherwise, your talents may go unused and your resources may be squandered.

So, as you plan for your future, remember this: life's greatest rewards are unlikely to fall into your lap; to the contrary, your greatest accomplishments will probably require lots of work and plenty of self-discipline. And it's up to you to behave accordingly.

A spiritual life without discipline is impossible.
Discipline is the other side of discipleship.
The practice of a spiritual discipline makes us
more sensitive to the small, gentle voice of God.

Henri Nouwen

PRIORITIES FOR MY LIFE

A disciplined lifestyle gives you more control: The more disciplined you become, the more you can take control over your life (which, by the way, is far better than letting your life take control over you).

TIMELESS WISDOM FOR GODLY LIVING

The secret of a happy life is to delight in duty. When duty becomes delight, then burdens become blessings.

Warren Wiersbe

Discipline is the refining fire by which talent becomes ability.

Roy L. Smith

Simply stated, self-discipline is obedience to God's Word and willingness to submit everything in life to His will, for His ultimate glory.

John MacArthur

If one examines the secret behind a championship football team, a magnificent orchestra, or a successful business, the principal ingredient is invariably discipline.

James Dobson

> *I discipline my body and make it my slave.*
> 1 Corinthians 9:27 NASB

The alternative to discipline is disaster.

Vance Havner

MORE WORDS FROM GOD'S WORD

God hasn't invited us into a disorderly, unkempt life but into something holy and beautiful—as beautiful on the inside as the outside.

1 Thessalonians 4:7 MSG

Discipline yourself for the purpose of godliness.

1 Timothy 4:7 NASB

My son, do not despise the chastening of the Lord, nor be discouraged when you are rebuked by Him.

Hebrews 12:5 NKJV

No discipline seems pleasant at the time, but painful. Later on, however, it produces a harvest of righteousness and peace for those who have been trained by it.

Hebrews 12:11 NIV

MY PRIORITIES FOR LIFE

Check Your Priority

High   Med.   Low

I value the rewards of a disciplined lifestyle.

—   —   —

I understand the importance of disciplining myself emotionally, mentally, spiritually, and physically.

—   —   —

I believe that when I work hard, my hard work is usually rewarded.

—   —   —

Entrusting Our Hopes to God

The lines of purpose in your lives never grow slack,
tightly tied as they are to your future in heaven, kept taut by hope.

Colossians 1:5 MSG

On the darkest days of our lives, we may be confronted with an illusion that seems very real indeed: the illusion of hopelessness. Try though we might, we simply can't envision a solution to our problems—and we fall into the darkness of despair. During these times, we may question God—His love, His presence, even His very existence. Despite God's promises, despite Christ's love, and despite our many blessings, we may envision little or no hope for the future. These dark days can be dangerous times for us and for our loved ones.

If you find yourself falling into the spiritual traps of worry and discouragement, seek the encouraging words of fellow Christians, and the healing touch of Jesus. After all, it was Christ who promised, "These things I have spoken unto you, that in me ye might have peace. In the world ye shall have tribulation: but be of good cheer; I have overcome the world" (John 16:33 KJV).

Can you place your future into the hands of a loving and all-knowing God? Can you live amid the uncertainties of today, knowing that God has dominion over all your tomorrows? Can you summon the faith to trust God in good times and hard times? If you can, you are wise and you are blessed.

Once you've made the decision to trust God completely, it's time to get busy. The willingness to take action—even if the outcome of that action is uncertain—is an effective way to combat hopelessness. When you decide to roll up your sleeves and begin solving your own problems, you'll feel empowered, and you may see the first real glimmer of hope.

If you're waiting for someone else to solve your problems, or if you're waiting for God to patch things up by Himself, you may become impatient, despondent, or both. But when you stop waiting and start working, God has a way of pitching in and finishing the job. The advice of American publisher Cyrus Curtis still rings true: "Believe in the Lord and He will do half the work—the last half."

So, today and every day, ask God for these things: clear perspective, mountain-moving faith, and the courage to do what needs doing. After all, no problem is too big for God—not even yours.

When you say a situation or a person is hopeless,
you are slamming the door in the face of God.

Charles Allen

PRIORITIES FOR MY LIFE

Don't give up hope: Other people have experienced the same kind of hard times you may be experiencing now. They made it, and so can you.

TIMELESS WISDOM FOR GODLY LIVING

Many things are possible for the person who has hope. Even more is possible for the person who has faith. And still more is possible for the person who knows how to love. But everything is possible for the person who practices all three virtues.

Brother Lawrence

Nothing in this world is more fundamental for success in life than hope, and this star pointed to our only source of true hope: Jesus Christ.

D. James Kennedy

What oxygen is to the lungs, such is hope to the meaning of life.

Emil Brunner

Let us hold fast the confession of our hope without wavering, for He who promised is faithful.
Hebrews 10:23 NASB

Oh, remember this: There is never a time when we may not hope in God. Whatever our necessities, however great our difficulties, and though to all appearance help is impossible, yet our business is to hope in God, and it will be found that it is not in vain.

George Mueller

MORE WORDS FROM GOD'S WORD

This hope we have as an anchor of the soul, a hope both sure and steadfast.

Hebrews 6:19 NASB

Full of hope, you'll relax, confident again; you'll look around, sit back, and take it easy.

Job 11:18 MSG

Be of good courage, and he shall strengthen your heart, all ye that hope in the LORD.

Psalm 31:24 KJV

Be joyful in hope, patient in affliction, faithful in prayer.

Romans 12:12 NIV

MY PRIORITIES FOR LIFE

I believe that genuine hope begins with hope in a sovereign God.

I have found that action is an antidote to worry.

I believe that God offers me "a peace that passes understanding," and I desire to accept God's peace.

Check Your Priority		
High	Med.	Low
—	—	—
—	—	—
—	—	—

He Rules

Can you understand the secrets of God?
His limits are higher than the heavens; you cannot reach them!
They are deeper than the grave; you cannot understand them!
His limits are longer than the earth and wider than the sea.

Job 11:7-9 NCV

The heart of God, like the hand of God, is sovereign: it reigns over all God's creation, including You. Your challenge is to recognize God's sovereignty and live in accordance with His commandments. Sometimes, of course, this is easier said than done.

Proverbs 3:6 gives you guidance: "In all your ways acknowledge Him, and He shall direct your paths." When you think about it, the words in this verse make a powerful promise: If you acknowledge God's sovereignty over every aspect of your life, He will guide your path. That's an important promise. So, as you prayerfully consider the path that God intends for you to take, here are things you should do: You should study His Word and be ever-watchful for His signs. You should associate with fellow believers who will encourage your spiritual growth. You should listen carefully to that inner voice that speaks to you in the quiet moments of your daily devotionals. And, as you continually seek God's unfolding purpose for your life, you should be patient.

Your Heavenly Father may not always reveal himself as quickly as you would like. But rest assured: God is sovereign, God is here, God is love, and God intends to use you in wonderful, unexpected ways. He desires to lead you along a path of His choosing. Your challenge is to watch, to listen, to learn . . . and to follow.

You will feel that He must rule and control each day.
All of life and conversation must be in the Spirit. My prayer,
my faith, my fellowship with the Father, and all my work in
God's service, must be completely under His sway.
As the Spirit of Holiness, He is the Spirit of my sanctification.

Andrew Murray

PRIORITIES FOR MY LIFE

God is in control and can take care of every problem you have. Vance Havner writes, "When we get to a place where it can't be done unless God does it, God will do it!" Enough said.

TIMELESS WISDOM FOR GODLY LIVING

Depositing our faith in Jesus Christ means God is now responsible for us, because He has purchased us.

Franklin Graham

When terrible things happen, there are two choices, and only two: We can trust God, or we can defy Him. We believe that God is God, He's still got the whole world in His hands and knows exactly what He's doing, or we must believe that He is not God and that we are at the awful mercy of mere chance.

Elisabeth Elliot

God has charged Himself with full responsibility for our eternal happiness and stands ready to take over the management of our lives the moment we turn in faith to Him.

A. W. Tozer

> *For now we see indistinctly, as in a mirror,*
> *but then face to face. Now I know in part,*
> *but then I will know fully, as I am fully known.*
> 1 Corinthians 13:12 Holman CSB

He proves His sovereignty, not by intervening constantly and preventing these events, but by ruling and overruling them so that even tragedies end up accomplishing His ultimate purposes.

Warren Wiersbe

MORE WORDS FROM GOD'S WORD

However, each one must live his life in the situation the Lord assigned when God called him.

1 Corinthians 7:17 Holman CSB

O Lord, you have examined my heart and know everything about me. You know when I sit down or stand up. You know my every thought when far away. You chart the path ahead of me and tell me where to stop and rest.

Psalm 139:1-3 NLT

He is the Lord. He will do what He thinks is good.

1 Samuel 3:18 Holman CSB

Commit your activities to the Lord and your plans will be achieved.

Proverbs 16:3 Holman CSB

MY PRIORITIES FOR LIFE

I believe God is in control of the universe and my universe.

I believe I may not understand "why" but I can still ask "What should I do now, God?"

I believe God is loving and just, and one day everything will be made right.

Check Your Priority		
High	Med.	Low
—	—	—
—	—	—
—	—	—

Today's Work

In all the work you are doing, work the best you can.
Work as if you were doing it for the Lord, not for people.

Colossians 3:23 NCV

Have you acquired the habit of doing first things first, or are you one of those people who put off important work until the last minute? The answer to this simple question will help determine how well you do your work and how much fun you have doing it.

God's Word teaches the value of hard work. In his second letter to the Thessalonians, Paul warns, " ...if any would not work, neither should he eat" (3:10 KJV). And the Book of Proverbs proclaims, "One who is slack in his work is brother to one who destroys" (18:9 NIV). In short, God has created a world in which diligence is rewarded and laziness is not. So, whatever it is that you choose to do, do it with commitment, excitement, and vigor. And remember this: Hard work is not simply a proven way to get ahead, it's also part of God's plan for you.

Norman Vincent Peale said, "Think enthusiastically about everything, especially your work." If you're wise, you'll take that advice. When you do, you'll soon discover that the old saying is true: attitude determines altitude.

You have countless opportunities to accomplish great things for your God, for your family, and for yourself—but you should not expect the work to be easy. So pray as if everything depended upon God, but work as if everything depended upon you. When you do, you should expect very big payoffs. Why? Because when you and God become partners in your work, amazing things are bound to happen.

Dear Lord, let us pray for our daily bread,
but let us not be afraid to hunt for our corn-pone
with sweat running down the hoe handle.

Sam Jones

He did it with all his heart. So he prospered.

2 Chronicles 31:21 NKJV

PRIORITIES FOR MY LIFE

Have faith and get to work: Earning great things usually requires work and lots of it, which is perfectly fine with God. After all, He knows that you're up to the task, and He has big plans for you. Very big plans . . .

TIMELESS WISDOM FOR GODLY LIVING

If you want to reach your potential, you need to add a strong work ethic to your talent.

John Maxwell

There was never a person who did anything worth doing that did not receive more than he gave.

Henry Ward Beecher

Chiefly the mold of a man's fortune is in his own hands.

Francis Bacon

The higher the ideal, the more work is required to accomplish it. Do not expect to become a great success in life if you are not willing to work for it.

Father Flanagan

Be strong and brave, and do the work. Don't be afraid or discouraged, because the Lord God, my God, is with you. He will not fail you or leave you."
1 Chronicles 28:20 NCV

People who work for money only are usually miserable, because there is no fulfillment and no meaning to what they do.

Dave Ramsey

MORE WORDS FROM GOD'S WORD

But thanks be to God, who gives us the victory through our Lord Jesus Christ. Therefore, my beloved brethren, be steadfast, immovable, always abounding in the work of the Lord, knowing that your labor is not in vain in the Lord.

1 Corinthians 15:57-58 NKJV

But one thing I do: Forgetting what is behind and straining toward what is ahead, I press on toward the goal to win the prize for which God has called me heavenward in Christ Jesus.

Philippians 3:13-14 NIV

Then He said to His disciples, "The harvest truly is plentiful, but the laborers are few."

Matthew 9:37 NKJV

MY PRIORITIES FOR LIFE

I understand the need to work diligently, consistently, and enthusiastically.

I seek to associate with hardworking, enthusiastic people.

I understand that I'm personally responsible for the quality of my work.

Check Your Priority		
High	Med.	Low
—	—	—
—	—	—
—	—	—

The Power of Encouragement

So encourage each other and give each other strength,
just as you are doing now.

1 Thessalonians 5:11 NCV

The 118th Psalm reminds us, "This is the day which the Lord hath made; we will rejoice and be glad in it" (v. 24 KJV). As we rejoice in this day that the Lord has given us, let us remember that an important part of today's celebration is the time we spend celebrating others. Each day provides countless opportunities to encourage others and to praise their good works. When we do, we not only spread seeds of joy and happiness, we also follow the commandments of God's Holy Word.

In his letter to the Ephesians, Paul writes, "Do not let any unwholesome talk come out of your mouths, but only what is helpful for building others up according to their needs, that it may benefit those who listen" (4:29 NIV). This passage reminds us that, as Christians, we are instructed to choose our words carefully so as to build others up through wholesome, honest encouragement. How can we build others up? By celebrating their victories and their accomplishments. As the old saying goes, "When someone does something good, applaud—you'll make two people happy."

Today, look for the good in others and celebrate the good that you find. When you do, you'll be a powerful force of encouragement in the world . . . and a worthy servant to your God.

A lot of people have gone further than they thought they could because someone else thought they could.

Zig Ziglar

But encourage one another day after day,
as long as it is still called "Today," so that none of you
will be hardened by the deceitfulness of sin.

Hebrews 3:13 NASB

PRIORITIES FOR MY LIFE

And seldom is heard a discouraging word . . . If it's good enough for "Home on the Range," it's good enough for your home, too. Make certain that your little abode is a haven of encouragement for every member of your family. You do so by checking your gripes and disappointments at the front door . . . and encouraging everybody else to do likewise!

TIMELESS WISDOM FOR GODLY LIVING

Perhaps we have been guilty of speaking against someone and have not realized how it may have hurt them. Then when someone speaks against us, we suddenly realize how deeply such words hurt, and we become sensitive to what we have done.

Theodore Epp

The secret of success is to find a need and fill it, to find a hurt and heal it, to find somebody with a problem and offer to help solve it.

Robert Schuller

The truest help we can render an afflicted man is not to take his burden from him, but to call out his best energy, that he may be able to bear the burden himself.

Phillips Brooks

He comes alongside us when we go through hard times, and before you know it, he brings us alongside someone else who is going through hard times so that we can be there for that person just as God was there for us.

2 Corinthians 1:4 MSG

God grant that we may not hinder those who are battling their way slowly into the light.

Oswald Chambers

MORE WORDS FROM GOD'S WORD

Encourage each other. Live in harmony and peace. Then the God of love and peace will be with you.

2 Corinthians 13:11 NLT

So don't lose a minute in building on what you've been given, complementing your basic faith with good character, spiritual understanding, alert discipline, passionate patience, reverent wonder, warm friendliness, and generous love, each dimension fitting into and developing the others.

2 Peter 1:5-7 MSG

Watch the way you talk. Let nothing foul or dirty come out of your mouth. Say only what helps, each word a gift.

Ephesians 4:29 MSG

MY PRIORITIES FOR LIFE

I believe that God wants me to encourage other people.

I carefully think about the words I speak so that every word might be a "gift of encouragement" to others.

My words reflect my heart. I will guard my heart so that my words will be pleasing to God.

Check Your Priority		
High	Med.	Low
—	—	—
—	—	—
—	—	—

Making Forgiveness
a High Priority

Be even-tempered, content with second place, quick to forgive an offense.
Forgive as quickly and completely as the Master forgave you.
And regardless of what else you put on, wear love. It's your basic,
all-purpose garment. Never be without it.

Colossians 3:13-14 MSG

D o you value the role that forgiveness can play in your life? Hopefully so. But even if you're a dedicated believer, you may have a difficult time forgiving those who have hurt you. If you're one of those folks who, despite your best intentions, has a difficult time forgiving and forgetting, you are not alone.

Life would be much simpler if we humans could forgive people "once and for all" and be done with it. But forgiveness is seldom that easy. For most people, the decision to forgive is straightforward, but the process of forgiving is more difficult. Forgiveness is a journey that requires effort, time, perseverance, and prayer.

Sometimes, it's not "the other person" whom you need to forgive; it's yourself. If you've made mistakes (And who among us hasn't?), perhaps you're continuing to bear a grudge against the person in the mirror. If so, here's a three-step process for resolving those feelings: 1. Stop the harmful behavior that is the source of your self-directed anger. 2. Seek forgiveness from God (and from any people whom you may have hurt). 3. Ask God to cleanse your heart of all bitterness and regret . . . and keep asking Him until your feelings of anger and regret are gone.

If there exists even one person, alive or dead, whom you have not forgiven (and that includes yourself), follow God's commandment: forgive that person today. And remember that bitterness, anger, and regret are not part of God's plan for your life. Forgiveness is.

Perhaps you need a refresher course in the art of forgiveness. If so, it's time to open your Bible and your heart. When you do, you'll discover that God can heal your broken spirit. Don't expect forgiveness to be easy or quick, but rest assured that with God as your partner, you can forgive . . . and you will.

The sequence of forgiveness and then repentance,
rather than repentance and then forgiveness,
is crucial for understanding the gospel of grace.

Brennan Manning

PRIORITIES FOR MY LIFE

Forgive . . . and keep forgiving! Sometimes, you may forgive someone once and then, at a later time, become angry at the very same person again. If so, you must forgive that person again and again . . . until it sticks!

TIMELESS WISDOM FOR GODLY LIVING

To forgive the incessant provocations of daily life—to keep on forgiving the bossy mother-in-law, the bullying husband, the nagging wife, the selfish daughter, the deceitful son—how can we do it? Only, I think, by remembering where we stand, by meaning our words when we say in our prayers each night, "Forgive us our trespasses as we forgive those that trespass against us." We are offered forgiveness on no other terms. To refuse it is to refuse God's mercy for ourselves. There is no hint of exceptions and God means what he says.

C. S. Lewis

I firmly believe a great many prayers are not answered because we are not willing to forgive someone.

D. L. Moody

Forgiving is a gift God has given us for healing ourselves before we are ready to help anyone else.

Dr. Lewis Smedes

> *Hatred stirs up trouble, but love forgives all wrongs.*
> Proverbs 10:12 NCV

Forgiveness is the antiseptic for our emotional wounds.

Floyd McClung, Jr.

MORE WORDS FROM GOD'S WORD

Be gentle with one another, sensitive. Forgive one another as quickly and thoroughly as God in Christ forgave you.

Ephesians 4:32 MSG

And forgive us our sins, for we ourselves also forgive everyone in debt to us. And do not bring us into temptation.

Luke 11:4 NKJV

Whenever you stand praying, forgive, if you have anything against anyone, so that your Father in heaven will also forgive you your transgressions.

Mark 11:25 NASB

Praise the Lord, I tell myself, and never forget the good things he does for me. He forgives all my sins and heals all my diseases.

Psalm 103:3 NLT

MY PRIORITIES FOR LIFE

For me, forgiveness is not optional; it is a commandment from God.

I consider forgiveness to be a way of liberating myself from the chains of the past.

Forgiving other people is one way of strengthening my relationship with God.

Check Your Priority		
High	Med.	Low
—	—	—
—	—	—
—	—	—

Kindness in Action

Be kind to each other, tenderhearted, forgiving one another,
just as God through Christ has forgiven you.

Ephesians 4:32 NLT

The noted American theologian Phillips Brooks advised, "Be such a man, and live such a life, that if every man were such as you, and every life a life like yours, this earth would be God's Paradise." One tangible way to make the world a more godly place is to spread kindness wherever we go.

For Christian believers, kindness is not an option, it is a commandment. In the Gospel of Matthew, Jesus declares, "In everything, therefore, treat people the same way you want them to treat you, for this is the Law and the Prophets" (Matthew 7:12 NASB). Jesus did not say, "In some things, treat people as you wish to be treated." And, He did not say, "From time to time, treat others with kindness." Christ said that we should treat others as we wish to be treated in everything. This, of course, is a tall order indeed, but as Christians, we are commanded to do our best.

Today, as you consider all the things that Christ has done in your life, honor Him by being a little kinder than necessary. Honor Him by slowing down long enough to say an extra word of encouragement to someone who needs it. Honor Him by picking up the phone and calling a distant friend . . . for no reason other than to say, "I'm thinking of you." Honor Christ by following His commandment and obeying the Golden Rule. He expects no less, and He deserves no less.

Be so preoccupied with good will that you
haven't room for ill will.

E. Stanley Jones

So, as those who have been chosen of God, holy and beloved,
put on a heart of compassion, kindness, humility,
gentleness and patience.

Colossians 3:12 NASB

PRIORITIES FOR MY LIFE

You can't just talk about it: In order to be a kind person, you must do kind things. Thinking about them isn't enough. So get busy! The day to start being a little more kind and generous is today!

TIMELESS WISDOM FOR GODLY LIVING

When you launch an act of kindness out into the crosswinds of life, it will blow kindness back to you.

Dennis Swanberg

A little kindly advice is better than a great deal of scolding.

Fanny Crosby

Let no one ever come to you without leaving better and happier. Be the living expression of God's kindness: kindness in your face, kindness in your eyes, kindness in your smile.

Mother Teresa

Make it a rule, and pray to God to help you to keep it, never, if possible, to lie down at night without being able to say: "I have made one human being at least a little wiser, or a little happier, or at least a little better this day."

Charles Kingsley

Carry each other's burdens,
and in this way you will fulfill the law of Christ.
Galatians 6:2 NIV

When you extend hospitality to others, you're not trying to impress people, you're trying to reflect God to them.

Max Lucado

MORE WORDS FROM GOD'S WORD

Finally, all of you should be of one mind, full of sympathy toward each other, loving one another with tender hearts and humble minds.

1 Peter 3:8 NLT

And may the Lord make you increase and abound in love to one another and to all.

1 Thessalonians 3:12 NKJV

A gentle answer turns away wrath, but a harsh word stirs up anger.

Proverbs 15:1 NIV

I tell you the truth, whatever you did for one of the least of these brothers of mine, you did for me.

Matthew 25:40 NIV

MY PRIORITIES FOR LIFE

As a Christian, I feel that it is my obligation to be kind to others.

In all my decisions I seek to apply the Golden Rule.

When I extend the hand of kindness to others, I feel that it is important for me to avoid public acclaim.

Check Your Priority		
High	Med.	Low
—	—	—
—	—	—
—	—	—

The Gift of Eternal Life

For God so loved the world, that he gave his only begotten Son,
that whosoever believeth in him should not perish,
but have everlasting life.

John 3:16 KJV

How marvelous it is that God became a man and walked among us. Had He not chosen to do so, we might feel removed from a distant Creator. But ours is not a distant God. Ours is a God who understands—far better than we ever could—the essence of what it means to be human.

God understands our hopes, our fears, and our temptations. He understands what it means to be angry and what it costs to forgive. He knows the heart, the conscience, and the soul of every person who has ever lived, including you. And God has a plan of salvation that is intended for you. Accept it. Accept God's gift through the person of His Son, Christ Jesus, and then rest assured: God walked among us so that you might have eternal life; amazing though it may seem, He did it for you.

As mere mortals, our vision for the future, like our lives here on earth, is limited. God's vision is not burdened by such limitations: His plans extend throughout all eternity. Thus, God's plans for you are not limited to the ups and downs of everyday life. Your Heavenly Father has bigger things in mind . . . much bigger things.

Let us praise the Creator for His priceless gift, and let us share the Good News with all who cross our paths. We return our Father's love by accepting His grace and by sharing His message and His love. When we do, we are blessed here on earth and throughout all eternity.

As you struggle with the inevitable hardships and occasional disappointments of life, remember that God has invited you to accept His abundance not only for today but also for all eternity. So keep things in perspective. Although you will inevitably encounter occasional defeats in this world, you'll have all eternity to celebrate the ultimate victory in the next.

Those of us who know the wonderful grace of redemption look forward to an eternity with God, when all things will be made new, when all our longings will at last find ultimate and final satisfaction.

Joseph Stowell

PRIORITIES FOR MY LIFE

What a friend you have in Jesus: Jesus loves you, and He offers you eternal life with Him in heaven. Welcome Him into your heart. Now!

TIMELESS WISDOM FOR GODLY LIVING

Someday you will read in the papers that Moody is dead. Don't you believe a word of it. At that moment I shall be more alive than I am now. I was born of the flesh in 1837, I was born of the spirit in 1855. That which is born of the flesh may die. That which is born of the Spirit shall live forever.

D. L. Moody

God dwells in eternity, but time dwells in God. He has already lived all our tomorrows as he has lived all our yesterdays.

A. W. Tozer

God did not spring forth from eternity; He brought forth eternity.

C. H. Spurgeon

The choices of time are binding in eternity.

Jack MacArthur

And this is the will of Him who sent Me, that everyone who sees the Son and believes in Him may have everlasting life; and I will raise him up at the last day.
John 6:40 NKJV

He who has no vision of eternity will never get a true hold of time.

Thomas Carlyle

MORE WORDS FROM GOD'S WORD

And this is the testimony: that God has given us eternal life, and this life is in His Son. He who has the Son has life; he who does not have the Son of God does not have life.

1 John 5:11-12 NKJV

These things I have written to you who believe in the name of the Son of God, that you may know that you have eternal life.

1 John 5:13 NKJV

Don't be troubled. You trust God, now trust in me. There are many rooms in my Father's home, and I am going to prepare a place for you. If this were not so, I would tell you plainly. When everything is ready, I will come and get you, so that you will always be with me where I am.

John 14:1-3 NLT

MY PRIORITIES FOR LIFE

I believe my eternity with God is secure because I believe in Jesus.

I have a responsibility to tell as many people as I can about the eternal life that Jesus offers.

I praise God and His Son for the gift of eternal life.

Check Your Priority		
High	Med.	Low
—	—	—
—	—	—
—	—	—

*The thing you should want most is
God's kingdom and doing what God wants.
Then all these other things you need
will be given to you.*

Matthew 6:33 NCV

TOPIC	TITLE	PAGE